OLD

General Editor:

R.N. Whybray

THE SECOND ISAIAH

224.106
W629s

THE
SECOND
ISAIAH

R.N.Whybray

JSOT Press

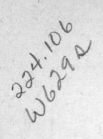

To Mary

Copyright © 1983 JSOT Press

Published by
JSOT Press
Department of Biblical Studies
The University of Sheffield
Sheffield S10 2TN
England

Printed in Great Britain
by Dotesios (Printers) Ltd.,
Bradford-on-Avon, Wiltshire.

British Library Cataloguing in Publication Data

Whybray, R.N.
    The Second Isaiah.—(Old Testament Guides,
    ISSN 0264-6498; 1)
    1. Bible. O.T. Isaiah—Criticism, interpretation,
    etc.
    I. Title   II. Series   fig.
    224'.1'06   BS1515.2

ISBN 0-905774-59-0

CONTENTS

PREFACE

This volume, like my commentary on Isaiah 40-66 in the *New Century Bible* series (1975) and my two monographs *The Heavenly Counsellor in Isaiah xl 13-14* (1971) and *Thanksgiving for a Liberated Prophet* (1978), is the outcome of constant preoccupation with the second half of the Book of Isaiah since I first prepared lectures on it in 1965. I believe that the view which has for many years been almost universally held, that chapters 40-55 are substantially the work of a single anonymous 'prophet of the Exile', remains valid and is likely to remain the view of the majority of scholars. At all events, students of these chapters will find it essential to familiarize themselves with this interpretation of 'The Second Isaiah' before moving on to grasp and assess new theories (such as those referred to in the bibliography to Chapter 1), since it will remain for a long time to come the starting-point for discussion of the subject.

University of Hull   R.N. Whybray
July 1981

INTRODUCTION

The sixteen chapters (40-55) of the Book of Isaiah usually known as Deutero-Isaiah or Second Isaiah make a particularly attractive starting-point for the student of the prophetical literature of the Old Testament because they comprise essentially the collected oracles of a single prophet. Such an extensive sequence of prophetical oracles almost uninterrupted by later additions is unparalleled in the Old Testament. In general, uncertainty about date and authorship is one of the greatest problems attending the study of the prophetical books. Almost every book contains material composed at a variety of times and added to an original body of prophecy in order to elaborate, modify or reinterpret its message. The task of separating this disparate material from an original core, and determining the limits, date and purpose of each subsequent addition is usually one of such difficulty that there is no consensus of opinion either about the character of the original message or about the subsequent stages by which the book reached its final form. When the student first realizes that no two scholars are agreed on these questions, he may easily despair of ever mastering the subject.

In the case of Isaiah 40-55 the comparative absence of these problems is not, however, due to any unwonted absence of complications in the composition of the Book of Isaiah as a whole. On the contrary, recent study of this book suggests that its redactional history may be more complex than that of any other prophetical book of the Old Testament. What makes chapters 40-55 easier for the beginner is the fact that, although when considered as a part of the whole book they present as difficult a problem as any other with regard to their relationship to the other fifty chapters, they manifest such a high degree of *internal* coherence that they can, and indeed must, be studied as a distinct body of literature, one which has been preserved virtually untouched by later hands and which is at the same time sufficiently substantial to enable the reader to form a clear impression of the function and teaching of a particular prophet, without the necessity of the complicated and uncertain process of stripping away layers of subsequent interpretation and reinterpretation. That prophet, as will be seen, was not the prophet Isaiah who lived and prophesied during the eighth century B.C., but a prophet whose name is unknown to us (hence the title 'Deutero-Isaiah') who lived and prophesied in Babylon during the sixth century B.C.

The view expressed in the preceding paragraphs about the unity of the authorship of chapters 40-55 does not, of course, exclude the possibility that the processes whereby these chapters reached their present form and became attached to the rest of the book may have left behind them some traces of editorial or redactional work. Some very recent study of them (e.g. that of Merendino) has shown a tendency to magnify the extent of this. Nevertheless the consistency of thought and language to be found throughout the book is so marked that the prevailing consensus seems likely to endure; and students tackling Deutero-Isaiah for the first time would do well to accept it at least as a working hypothesis before venturing into the technicalities of the most recent redactional studies.

There are other reasons why the study of these chapters is particularly rewarding. They are among the most important, and have been among the most influential, chapters in the entire Bible. They already exerted great theological influence within the Old Testament period, as the later Old Testament writings show. They played a crucial role in the development of some of the great themes of Jewish and Christian theology. In particular the Judaeo-Christian doctrine of God, as unique, as creator of all things, as Lord of history, as almighty, righteous, loving, merciful and holy and as Saviour and Redeemer of his people owes a great deal to the teaching of 'Deutero-Isaiah.' His role in the development of doctrine was not so much that of an innovator as of one who articulated with greater clarity than his predecessors the theological understanding of God and the world which he had inherited, and was the first to expound these themes coherently in their relation to one another. He has been called the greatest theologian of the Old Testament; and—although there are others who might lay claim to that title—he was certainly one of the most important theological teachers whose work is to be found there.

But in order to understand his message it must be realized that the teaching of theology was not, in his eyes, his primary task. He was a prophet, and a prophet for his own time: that is, he believed himself to be the messenger of Yahweh to his people in a time of crisis. In order to address himself to that crisis and to persuade his contemporaries that the true God was alive and both able and willing to redeem them from their present distress, he summoned all the resources of a powerful theological intellect. As a consequence, the importance of his theological teaching remained, and remains, long after that particular crisis in Israel's history is over and done with. So to have studied the prophecies of Deutero-Isaiah is to have greatly enhanced one's knowledge of the Old Testament and of Judaeo-Christian theology.

Deutero-Isaiah came relatively late in the succession of Israelite prophets. He cannot, therefore, be understood without some knowledge of his prophetic predecessors, nor indeed without some knowledge of Israel's earlier religious traditions, upon which his teaching is built. Moreover, as a prophet with a message for his own time, he cannot be understood without some knowledge of the history of his time. In the chapters which follow these facts will not be forgotten, and an attempt will be made to provide students who come to the study of Isaiah 40-55 early in their Old Testament studies with sufficient information to enable them to profit by this book. It must also be emphasized that this is not a commentary. Although a large number of passages will be discussed in some detail in relation to Deutero-Isaiah's teaching, it will be assumed that readers will have at their disposal not only the biblical text in a reliable translation, but also a reliable commentary.

Each chapter of this book concludes with a select bibliography entitled 'Further Reading.' Special attention has been paid to the listing of material in English giving fuller information than it has been possible to provide here. Much of the original work on Deutero-Isaiah, however, is to be found only in publications in other languages. Although many readers will be unable to consult these, it has been thought right to include some of the most important of them, particularly those whose authors are mentioned in the text of the book.

Notes on the Bibliographies

The following abbreviations are used:

BZAW	Beihefte zur *Zeitschrift für die Alttestamentliche Wissenschaft*
JSOT	*Journal for the Study of the Old Testament*
OTL	Old Testament Library
TB	Theologische Bücherei
VT	*Vetus Testamentum*
VT Suppl.	Supplements to *Vetus Testamentum*
ZAW	*Zeitschrift für die Alttestamentliche Wissenschaft*

Full details of the works cited are given on their first appearance in the Bibliographies. In subsequent references they are cited by the surname of the author only, or, if more than one work by the same author are cited, by surname and date of publication, e.g. 'Torrey,' 'Westermann (1964).'

An asterisk (*) indicates works most suitable for beginners.

Further Reading

Among the older commentaries in English *J. Skinner, *The Book of the Prophet Isaiah Chapters XL-LXVI* (Cambridge Bible), Cambridge: Cambridge University Press, 1917 is still useful. More recent commentaries in English include:

> *J. Muilenburg, *Isaiah Chapters 40-66* (Interpreter's Bible, vol. 5, New York and Nashville: Abingdon Press, 1956, 381-773) (especially sensitive to literary and stylistic matters)

> *C.R. North, *The Second Isaiah*, Oxford: Clarendon Press, 1964 (contains discussions of the Hebrew text, but can also be used by non-Hebraists)

> *C. Westermann, *Isaiah 40-66* (OTL), London: SCM Press / Philadelphia: Westminster Press, 1969

> *R.N. Whybray, *Isaiah 40-66* (New Century Bible), London: Oliphants, 1975 / Grand Rapids: Eerdmans, 1981

Two commentaries which differ from the view of the majority of modern scholars about the date and purpose of Isaiah 40-55 are:

> C.C. Torrey, *The Second Isaiah. A New Interpretation*, Edinburgh: T. & T. Clark, 1928

> J.D. Smart, *History and Theology in Second Isaiah. A Commentary on Isaiah 35, 40-66*, Philadelphia: Westminster Press, 1965 / London: Epworth Press, 1967

Of the older commentaries in German the most outstanding is B. Duhm, *Das Buch Jesaia* (Göttinger Handkommentar zum Alten Testament), Göttingen: Vandenhoeck & Ruprecht, first published in 1892. The fifth edition of 1968 is a reprint of the fourth edition of 1922. This commentary covers the whole of the Book of Isaiah.

More recent commentaries in languages other than English include:

> P.-E. Bonnard, *Le second Isaïe, son disciple et leurs éditeurs* (Etudes Bibliques), Paris: Gabalda, 1972

> K. Elliger, *Deuterojesaja* (Biblischer Kommentar, Altes Testament

XI/1), Neukirchen-Vluyn: Neukirchener Verlag, 1978 (A very full and useful commentary. This first volume covers only 40:1–45:7. The commentary will be completed by H.-J. Hermisson.)

G. Fohrer, *Das Buch Jesaja*, Band 3 (Zürcher Bibelkommentare), Zurich and Stuttgart: Zwingli Verlag, 1964

P. Volz, *Jesaja II* (Kommentar zum Alten Testament), Leipzig: Werner Scholl, 1932; reprinted at Hildesheim and New York: Georg Olms Verlag, 1974

For a fuller list of commentaries see the Bibliography in my commentary.

1

'DEUTERO-ISAIAH' AND THE BOOK OF ISAIAH

The Traditional View

Traditionally it was taken for granted that the whole Book of Isaiah consisted of the collected prophecies of one man, Isaiah the son of Amoz, who lived in Jerusalem, the capital of the kingdom of Judah, in the eighth century B.C. (1:1). However, in the period before the rise of modern criticism at the end of the eighteenth century A.D., questions about the date, authorship and provenance of the various prophetical books did not have the same importance as they have now. These books were regarded as the vehicles of a perennially relevant religious message whose validity was independent of the historical circumstances which had given rise to their composition. This attitude is well exemplified in the words of Ben Sira (Ecclus. 48:24-25) written in the second century B.C. in praise of the prophet Isaiah. After a reference to an incident in his life recorded in the first part of the book (Isa. 38:1-8) he continued:

> By the spirit of might he saw the last things,
>   and comforted those who mourned in Zion.
> He revealed what was to occur to the end of time,
>   and the hidden things before they came to pass.

These lines refer to the second half of the book: they are in fact mainly dependent for their phraseology on certain passages such as 48:5, 6; 51:3; 61:2, 3. Clearly Ben Sira attributed the entire book to the eighth-century prophet Isaiah. But the trend of his exegesis ('the last things,' 'the end of time') shows that it would have made no essential difference to his understanding of the book had Isaiah lived at some other time. What was important to him was that he had predicted a glorious future for God's people at the end of time.

The Prophet of the Exile

Since the end of the eighteenth century it has been increasingly recognized that all literature is to a large extent a reflection of the period in which it was written, and has been influenced by the circumstances in which the authors lived. In the Old Testament this is particularly true of the words of the prophets, who were not primarily authors in a purely literary sense, but men who believed themselves to have been called to proclaim urgent messages to their contemporaries. In studying the prophetical books, therefore, it is particularly important to set them, as far as this is possible, against their historical backgrounds. But at an early stage in the modern study of these books it became clear that more than one different historical situation might be reflected in a single book: that, for example, in the Book of Isaiah, some sections appear to reflect periods subsequent to the eighth century B.C. and can therefore not be the work of Isaiah. Already in the twelfth century A.D. the Jewish commentator Ibn Ezra had cautiously expressed doubts about the book's unity; but it was not until 1789 that J.C. Döderlein, following a suggestion made in 1783 by J.G. Eichhorn, put forward a definite theory that chapters 40-66 are an independent work, the work of an anonymous prophet who lived towards the end of the Babylonian Exile in the middle of the sixth century B.C. Later scholars, beginning with Bernhard Duhm in his commentary on the Book of Isaiah (1892), further divided chapters 40-66 into two separate works; but the thesis that nothing after chapter 39 can be attributed to the eighth-century prophet, and that chapters 40-66 cannot be pre-exilic has been almost universally accepted and remains the standard opinion up to the present time. The main arguments supporting this thesis may be grouped under three headings.

1. *Anonymity*. The name of Isaiah never occurs in the last twenty-seven chapters of the book. In the earlier chapters it occurs sixteen times: four times in chapters 1-13, twice in chapter 20, and ten times in chapters 37-39. Of these occurrences, three—1:1; 2:1; 13:1—are in editorial headings clearly intended to claim Isaiah's authorship for an extensive group of oracles which follow. The frequency and placing of these occurrences create a strong impression that chapters 1-39, although they undoubtedly contain some later material, once formed a book which laid claim to be, in itself, a complete 'Book of Isaiah.'

On the other hand the abrupt and total cessation of such references after chapter 39 suggests equally strongly that chapters 40-66 stand outside that earlier book: they contain nothing which claims Isaian authorship for them. They are, in fact, anonymous: no-one is named as their author, and—in contrast with the earlier chapters—there are no editorial headings providing information about date or authorship.

2. *Style.* Obviously a full appreciation of the stylistic characteristics of a literary text is not possible through the medium of a translation, though in the case of Isaiah 40-55 even an English translation conveys something of the change of mood which occurs at the beginning of chapter 40. The author certainly has some key phrases in common with his eighth-century predecessor, but these may be accounted for by a common Judaean religious tradition. Also a few passages in the first part of the book, notably chapter 35, can hardly be distinguished in style and mood from chapters 40-55, and may even be the work of the same author. But in general there is an unmistakable note of exultation and confidence which runs through these chapters and marks them out as quite distinctive. This expresses itself concretely in many ways: in the use of phraseology, vocabulary and imagery, in the skilful use of metre and in particular in the use of characteristic literary forms and stylistic devices, many of which will be discussed in Chapter 4 and elsewhere in this book.

3. *The historical situation.* The anonymity of chapters 40-55 (leaving aside chapters 56-66 for the present) and their distinctive style and mood suggest, then, that they form a unified prophetic corpus originally unrelated to the prophecies of Isaiah, which must be treated independently if its original purpose and significance are to be properly understood. This kind of approach has led, through a detailed study of the actual contents of each oracle, to the inescapable conclusion that these are prophecies not from the eighth century B.C. but from the sixth. The reasons leading to this conclusion will be set out in more detail in Chapter 2 of this book and will be further tested in the course of closer examination of the text in the chapters which follow. Here only a brief account of the main points is necessary.

The most obvious indication of a sixth-century date is provided by the occurrence of the name Cyrus in 44:28 and 45:1. There can be no possible doubt that this person, who is described in this passage (44:24-45:7) and also—without being specifically named—in other passages as a king and a great conqueror raised up by Yahweh to rescue Yahweh's people from captivity, is the sixth-century Persian king Cyrus the Great, the founder of the Persian Empire.

But the sixth-century date does not depend on these two references alone. It is a simple fact that the content of the prophet's message from start to finish is quite inappropriate to the circumstances of the eighth century B.C. but entirely appropriate when seen as a message to Jewish exiles in Babylonia in the sixth. It is clearly addressed to a group of people who have been exiled from their homeland by a conquering power, which also is referred to by name: Babylon. In four passages (43:14; 47; 48:14, 20) Babylon is spoken of by name in these terms, and this historical situation is confirmed in numerous other passages.

Chapters 40-55, then, would have made no sense in the eighth century, when the people of Jerusalem and Judah were still living at home under the rule of their own kings; when Babylon, far from being a great power, was—and remained until the fall of Assyria in the late seventh century B.C., long after the death of Isaiah—merely one of the cities of the Assyrian Empire; and when Cyrus had not yet been born and the Persian Empire did not yet exist. On the other hand, everything in these chapters makes good sense as the message of a sixth-century prophet to the Jewish exiles in Babylon.

It would be possible to add a further argument for a sixth-century date: that of the place of Deutero-Isaiah's teaching in the history of the development of religious thought in Israel. In other words, his theological teaching has strong affinities with other sixth-century Old Testament writings and presupposes the teaching of the eighth- and seventh-century prophets. However, arguments of this kind are less secure than the three put forward above, since they tend to assume that the development of thought proceeds necessarily in a straight line and that no thinker, however brilliant, can anticipate later developments. In the case of Deutero-Isaiah the three arguments set out above are quite sufficient to establish that these chapters come from the sixth and not the eighth century B.C.

Deutero-Isaiah and the Book of Isaiah

But what of chapters 56-66? There is no obvious break in the text after chapter 55, and it was not until 1892 that Duhm advanced the thesis that chapters 56-66 form a separate work, to which he gave the name 'Trito-Isaiah.' This is not the place for a discussion of the problems of Trito-Isaiah. It is sufficient here to say that Duhm's view has been generally, if not unanimously, accepted by critical scholarship. While opinions remain divided about the unity and date or dates of chapters 56-66, they do not reflect the same historical situation as that reflected by chapters 40-55. The admitted similarities of theme and language which exist between chapters 40-55 and some parts of chapters 56-66 are best explained by the hypothesis that the latter section of the book contains passages by authors who were trying to adapt the message of Deutero-Isaiah to the circumstances of a somewhat later generation.

Why were chapters 40-55 (and 56-66) added to the older collection of Isaiah's oracles? This was certainly not done accidentally. The Book of Isaiah in its present form is intended to give the impression that all the oracles which it contains are those of Isaiah himself. The final editors wished to invest these anonymous prophecies with the authority of a great and famous prophet, and at the same time to present a much more positive and hopeful version of his message than was conveyed by chapters 1-39 alone. This tendency in post-exilic times to 'brighten up' the sombre message of an earlier prophet by inserting into his oracles or appending to them positive promises of a bright future has affected other prophetical books of the Old Testament and is also to be found within chapters 1-39 of Isaiah itself. The procedure was particularly effective in the case of Deutero-Isaiah because there was already an affinity between the two prophets (not to speak of Trito-Isaiah) in their devotion to Jerusalem and its religious traditions. Deutero-Isaiah's specific references to the situation of his time could then be interpreted either in generalized terms —for example, the perennial need for 'comfort,' which Yahweh supplied—or symbolically (Babylon as the perennial enemy of God's people). There is no need to assume, as some scholars have done, the existence of a 'school' of Isaiah's followers perpetuating itself in every generation from the eighth to the sixth century B.C.

Further Reading

On the date, provenance, authorship, relationship to the Book of Isaiah as a whole, and internal unity of chapters 40-55 see the standard Introductions, especially:

*S.R. Driver, *An Introduction to the Literature of the Old Testament*, Edinburgh: T. & T. Clark, 8th edition, 1909, 230-46 (and subsequent editions) (The arguments put forward here are still accepted by the majority of scholars.)

*O. Eissfeldt, *The Old Testament. An Introduction*, Oxford: Basil Blackwell / New York: Harper and Row, 1965, 304, 332-8

*R.H. Pfeiffer, *Introduction to the Old Testament*, New York: Harper, 1948 / London: A. & C. Black, 1952, 415-6, 452-9

Other discussions of the subject are to be found in:

B.S. Childs, *Introduction to the Old Testament as Scripture*, London: SCM Press / Philadelphia, Fortress Press, 1979, 316-8 (see note below.)

The Interpreter's Dictionary of the Bible, Nashville and New York: Abingdon Press, vol. 2, 1962, article 'Isaiah,' 737-8

*Muilenburg, 382-6

*North (1964), 1-4

*Skinner, xv-xlv

A different view of these questions is to be found in:

U.E. Simon, *A Theology of Salvation. A Commentary on Isaiah 40-55*, London: SPCK, 1953, 1-25

Torrey, 3-110

In some recent studies theories of large-scale redactional expansions of the original oracles have been put forward which challenge the view expressed in this book and accepted by the great majority of scholars that Isa. 40-55 are substantially the work of a single prophet. It is too early to predict whether these new theories herald a change of direction in scholarly opinion. They are to be found in the following:

H.-C. Schmitt, 'Prophetie und Schultheologie im Deuterojesajabuch,' *ZAW* 91 (1979) 43-61

R.P. Merendino, *Der Erste und der Letzte* (VT Suppl. 31), Leiden: Brill, 1981

An even more extreme view is expressed in two books which challenge the entire thesis of a single anonymous prophet:

> J.M. Vincent, *Studien zur literarischen Eigenart und zur geistigen Heimat von Jesaja, Kap. 40-55* (Beiträge zur biblischen Exegese und Theologie, 5), Frankfurt and Berne: Peter Lang, 1977

> J.H. Eaton, *Festal Drama in Deutero-Isaiah*, London: SPCK, 1979

Neither of these works, however, deals adequately with the contrary evidence.

The literary style of Isaiah 40-55 is described in:

> *Muilenburg, 386-93

> *Pfeiffer, 462-70

N.B. Childs's reconstruction (325-38) of the reasons for the incorporation of chapters 40-55 (and 56-66) into the final Book of Isaiah is of considerable interest. However, his conclusion that critical study ought to confine itself to this final 'canonical shape' and not go behind it to interpret the component parts of the books in terms of their various historical contexts is a judgement of a different order which does not necessarily follow from his analysis.

2

THE HISTORICAL
BACKGROUND

In 587 B.C. the tiny kingdom of Judah, the survivor of the two kingdoms into which the united kingdom of Israel had been split at the death of Solomon, succumbed to the military power of the neo-Babylonian Empire. Despite its traditional confidence in its special relationship with its God Yahweh, but in accordance with the predictions of prophets such as Jeremiah and Ezekiel, its capital Jerusalem and the other cities were laid waste, the temple at Jerusalem pillaged and burnt, the king and many high officials executed, and the whole apparatus of government brought to an end. Of those who survived, many, including the former leaders of the nation, were deported to Babylonia. A substantial proportion of the population, however (the accounts in 2 Kings 25 and in Jer. 39 and 52 do not state how many), remained.

The deportation of 587 B.C. was only one of several. There had been a previous one, following an earlier Babylonian campaign, in 597 B.C. (2 Kings 24:10-17), and another was to follow in 581 B.C. (Jer. 52:28-30).

Deutero-Isaiah's prophetic ministry was exercised during the period following 587 B.C., which is generally known as the Babylonian Exile, that is during the half century between the fall of Jerusalem and the conquest of Babylon by the Persian Cyrus in 539 B.C. His familiarity with the Babylonian scene establishes beyond reasonable doubt that he was one of the exiles in Babylon. His career, however, falls in the latter part of the period. As has already been noted, he was familiar with the name of Cyrus, whom he regarded as the man destined by Yahweh to conquer Babylon and to release the Jewish exiles. Throughout his extant oracles he regarded these events as imminent. But in order to understand the situation in which he exercised his ministry it is necessary to survey the history of the preceding half century.

In 587 B.C. the power of the neo-Babylonian Empire was at its peak. But it was not destined to be of long duration. Nebuchadnezzar, the conqueror of Jerusalem, was its greatest king; and a decline began soon after his death in 562 B.C. In 556 B.C., after a period of confusion, the Babylonians placed on the throne one Nabû-na'id (Nabonidus), a native of Harran. About Nabonidus's capabilities there is some doubt, as the extant Babylonian texts differ in their assessments of him. But there is no doubt that he caused divisions in the state by his antagonism towards the cult of Marduk, the patron deity of the city of Babylon, and its powerful priesthood. He revived the cults of other gods whose worship had long since been discontinued in Babylon and had a special devotion to the god Sin, the god of his native city Harran.

Then for about eight years (552-545) Nabonidus, for some reason which has never been satisfactorily explained, left the capital, Babylon, and set up his court in the oasis of Teima in the north Arabian desert. Whatever reasons there may have been for this move, it was an unfortunate decision. Apart from the difficulty of administering the empire from such a remote place and at a time when the Medes and then the Persians were already posing a severe threat to the empire's survival, the king's absence from Babylon meant that during these years it was impossible to celebrate the rites of the New Year Festival, in which the king played an essential role. The failure to perform these rites, on which the good fortune, if not the very existence, of Babylon was believed to depend, was regarded in Babylon as a terrible calamity, and did much to undermine confidence.

The external menace to the empire had begun with the increasing power of the people known as the Medes. These had formerly been allies of Babylon, and it was with their help that the Babylonians had overthrown Assyria. But they then began to threaten the Babylonian Empire itself. Nabonidus, taking them to be the main threat to his empire, allied himself with Cyrus, king of Persia, against them; but in 550 B.C. Cyrus, who was a vassal king within the Median Empire, defeated the Median army without Babylonian assistance and found himself master of the Median Empire.

Nabonidus now realised that it was the Persians who were the real enemy. He desperately made an alliance with the only other two powers of consequence at that time, Egypt, then ruled by Amasis, and Lydia in western Asia Minor, whose king was Croesus. But in 547 B.C. Cyrus conquered Lydia. In 545 Nabonidus returned to Babylon, and the celebration of the New Year Festival was resumed. In the years which followed Cyrus was absent from the scene, occupied with conquests elsewhere. But in 539 his army arrived at the gates of Babylon. Cyrus now claimed to be the deliverer of the population from Nabonidus, and to be the true patron of their god Marduk whom Nabonidus had neglected. He had not miscalculated. The citizens of Babylon surrendered without a struggle and welcomed the conqueror, who took the titles of a Babylonian king and restored Marduk to his traditional position of honour. The neo-Babylonian Empire had come to an end, swallowed up in the greater Persian Empire. The city of Babylon continued to flourish, but now as a mere provincial city.

During this time the Jewish exiles in Babylon seem to have been well aware of the trend of political and military events. No doubt they wondered what difference, if any, the substitution of Persian rule for Babylonian would make to them, though they may have been aware that Cyrus, unlike the Assyrians and the Babylonians, did not make use of mass deportations as an instrument of policy. Most of them no doubt kept their thoughts to themselves during the last years of the Babylonian Empire. Deutero-Isaiah, however, did not. The meteoric career of Cyrus made a profound impression on him, and he delivered a number of oracles in which he predicted that Cyrus would overthrow Babylon and release the Jewish exiles (41:2-4; 41:25; 44:28; 45:1-6; 45:13; 46:11; 48:14-15). In one respect, however, he was mistaken: he thought that Cyrus would destroy the city of Babylon (see especially chapter 47). He did not. He made it more splendid than ever. But he did allow the Jewish exiles to return home if they wished, though not in the triumphant manner which Deutero-Isaiah expected.

Cyrus

Finally it is necessary to describe in more detail the meteoric career of Cyrus which Deutero-Isaiah followed with such enthusiasm.

When Cyrus was born, his people, the Persians, were a subject people within the Median Empire. The Medes and the Persians were closely related peoples of Aryan stock who had migrated southwards from the plains of southern Russia some centuries earlier: they first appear in Assyrian annals of the ninth century B.C. The Median Empire at the time of Cyrus's birth was extremely extensive, covering roughly the area of modern Iran together with part of ancient Assyria and northern Mesopotamia and a large part of Asia Minor, which had fallen to them when together with the Babylonians they had dismembered the Assyrian Empire at the end of the seventh century B.C.

Cyrus's father was king of Anshan, a small vassal kingdom east of the Tigris and north of the Persian Gulf, an area which had once been part of the kingdom of Elam and is now part of south-west Iran. When he succeeded his father in 559 B.C. Cyrus immediately set out to free the Persians from Median control. Very soon he had united all the Persian tribes. Then came his alliance with Babylon, which he saw as an opportunity to attack the Medes. In 550 B.C., as has already been stated, he succeeded in his aim. As the result of a battle during which a large part of the Median army changed sides, the Median king, Astyages, fell into his hands together with his empire.

The Persian Empire was now seen by the other powers of the area, Lydia, Babylon and Egypt, to be a dangerous enemy. But it was already too late to stop Cyrus. He first attacked Lydia in Asia Minor. In 547 he captured Sardis, the capital, and gained control not only of Lydia but also of the Greek cities in western Asia Minor. During the next few years he turned his attention to the east. He completed the conquest of the great Persian plateau as far as the borders of India in the east, and in the north-east subdued what is now Afghanistan, almost to the borders of China and well into southern Russia, as far as Samarkand. By these eastern conquests alone he more than doubled the extent of his empire.

In 540 B.C. Cyrus returned to the west. He invaded Mesopotamia and, after winning a battle in southern Babylonia, burned down the city of Akkad. The Babylonian troops were now thoroughly demoralised, and after a further battle Babylon received him as a conqueror.

The historical background outlined above makes it possible to determine within fairly narrow limits the period of the prophetical activity of Deutero-Isaiah, and also sheds light on the interpretation of some of his oracles. Cyrus's name and reputation, and the danger which he represented to the Babylonian power, are unlikely to have been familiar to the ordinary inhabitants of Babylon, who included the Jewish exiles, before his victory over the Medes in 550 B.C. But after that date his name will have been a household word. From 550 onwards Deutero-Isaiah's prediction of the imminent fall of Babylon and his glorification of Cyrus as a great conqueror and as the deliverer of the Jews, though extremely dangerous to the prophet's personal safety, would have seemed increasingly realistic. His oracles must therefore have been delivered within the years 550-539 B.C., and probably towards the end of that period.

It is not possible to go beyond this and to assign dates to the individual oracles. There is a certain differentiation of themes between chapters 40-48 and 49-55, but there is no evidence that this corresponds to chronological considerations. The attempts which have been made to discover a chronological sequence for the oracles on the basis of particular phrases within them betray an over-literal interpretation due to a failure to appreciate the nature of poetical language. Nor does the view that some of the oracles were addressed after 539 B.C. to exiles who had already returned to Palestine or were on their way home carry conviction. Here again poetical language, which in the case of Hebrew poetry often refers to future events as if they had already occurred (the so-called 'prophetic perfect' or 'perfect of certainty') has led to misunderstanding.

Further Reading

For the historical background see any of the following:

*J. Bright, *A History of Israel* (OTL), London: SCM Press / Philadelphia: Westminster Press, 2nd edition, 1972, 323-363

J.H. Hayes and J.M. Miller (ed.), *Israelite and Judaean History* (OTL), London: SCM Press / Philadelphia: Westminster Press, 1977, 469-86, 516-20

*S. Herrmann, *A History of Israel in Old Testament Times*, London: SCM Press / Philadelphia: Fortress Press, 1975, 274-96

*M. Noth, *The History of Israel*, London: A. & C. Black, 2nd edition / New York: Harper and Row, 1960, 280-306

For some relevant extra-biblical texts see:

J.B. Pritchard (ed.), *Ancient Near Eastern Texts Relating to the Old Testament*, Princeton: Princeton University Press, 1950, 305-7, 308-16

*D.W. Thomas (ed.), *Documents from Old Testament Times*, London and Edinburgh: Nelson / New York: Harper and Row, 1958, 84-94

3

DEUTERO-ISAIAH AND HIS PROPHETIC MISSION

Deutero-Isaiah and Earlier Prophecy

The student who comes to Deutero-Isaiah with some knowledge of the great eighth-century prophets Amos, Hosea, Micah and Isaiah may well have formed the impression that the main task of a Hebrew prophet was the proclamation of divine judgement upon a sinful nation. This impression may remain even after a study of Jeremiah and Ezekiel, who lived to see the fulfilment of that message of judgement in the events of 587 B.C., but who were able to discern more clearly than their predecessors the promise of some kind of hope for the future beyond the disaster. Whatever future hopes can safely be attributed to any of these prophets, it remains a fact that in every case their message was first of all one of divine anger and imminent judgement. But if these were true prophets, how can Deutero-Isaiah be reckoned among them? For in the teaching of Deutero-Isaiah the note of future judgement on Israel is wholly absent. His whole message was one of reassurance: of God's unlimited good will towards his people and of his determination to lose no time in restoring them to happiness and prosperity. Was not this message identical with that of the *false* prophets of Jeremiah's time, who had prophesied '"Peace, peace," when there was no peace' (Jer. 6:14), and had persisted in their foolish confidence even after the first deportation had taken place (Jer. 29:8-9)?

That in prophesying a bright future for Israel Deutero-Isaiah was reiterating the message of the false prophets is a fact. But to class him as one of them rather than as a successor of the great prophets of judgement would be totally to misunderstand the nature of Israelite prophecy. For the essence of Israelite prophecy resides not in its specific contents but in the source of inspiration to which it lays claim.

A prophet of Yahweh, though he might have other, secondary functions, such as warning or exhorting his hearers or giving explanatory comment in his own words, was first and foremost a messenger or mouthpiece of Yahweh, chosen by him to reproduce faithfully what he wished to say to his people—or to some particular individual or group of persons—at a particular moment. This claim is most clearly expressed in the so-called 'messenger-formula' 'Thus has Yahweh said,' a phrase which was regularly used by Deutero-Isaiah, as it had been by earlier prophets, to introduce his oracles. This messenger-formula corresponds to ordinary diplomatic usage such as we find, for example, in the opening words of the Assyrian envoy's message to Hezekiah: 'Thus has the great king, the king of Assyria, said' (Isa. 36:4).

The difference between Deutero-Isaiah's message and that of the earlier prophets of judgement does not, therefore, necessarily have anything to do with his own personal ideas or hopes. It does not mark him out as a false prophet, buoying up the people's wishful thinking with false optimism. As far as he was concerned the new message to be delivered was the consequence of a change in Yahweh's own intentions towards his people. The judgement announced by the pre-exilic prophets had been carried out and belonged to the past. Now after an interval of about forty years Yahweh had decided that the time had come for a new beginning.

That Deutero-Isaiah was indeed a true successor of the prophets of judgement is confirmed by the fact that his assessment of the cause of the national disaster is the same as theirs. The keynote of his message is that the time of servitude is over because Israel has now received from Yahweh's hand a fully adequate punishment for its sins (40:2). Unlike the false prophets, Deutero-Isaiah, in announcing Yahweh's change of heart, does not deny or minimize Israel's guilt, but recognizes that its punishment was just.

Deutero-Isaiah never refers to himself by the title 'prophet' (*nābî'*), nor does he speak of himself as 'prophesying.' His failure to use these terms, however, does not affect the claim that he was a prophet in the same sense as the pre-exilic prophets, since they also had tended to avoid them: Isaiah, for example, never spoke of himself in this way, although the editors of the Book of Isaiah do so. That he believed himself to belong to the company of the prophets is shown in many ways. The use of the messenger-formula, with its implicit claim that the speaker is transmitting words of Yahweh originally spoken to him

alone, is in itself sufficient proof of this. He also resembles earlier
prophets in other ways: in his consciousness of having received a
specific call from Yahweh to his prophetic ministry, in many of the
modes of expression and literary figures which he employs, and in his
use of traditional prophetic themes, particularly those associated
with Isaiah. There are also, not surprisingly, parallels with the messages of his nearest predecessors Jeremiah and Ezekiel, who in the
earlier part of the Exile had faced situations not unlike his own.
These matters will be more fully explored in Chapters 4 and 5 of this
book.

Another feature which Deutero-Isaiah's ministry had in common
with that of his predecessors was that he faced a problem of credibility:
of persuading a sceptical audience that he was a true prophet of
Yahweh. Lack of recognition can almost be said to have been a
hallmark of the Israelite prophet. This failure on the part of a prophet's
audience to accept his claim to be a true prophet was not simply due
to a wilful refusal on their part to listen to the word of Yahweh.
There was a conflict among the voices which claimed their attention.
Since both true and false prophets claimed to speak in Yahweh's
name, the problem of distinguishing the true prophet was a real one.
In the time of Jeremiah, about which we have the fullest information,
the false prophets' message that Yahweh would stand by his people
and turn away the threatened disaster was plausibly based on traditional beliefs, while Jeremiah with his message of woe was condemned
as a false prophet and a traitor. Attempts were made to establish
criteria for distinguishing the true message from the false, but these
all proved unsatisfactory. Once the Exile had begun the prevailing
mood changed from one of over-confidence to one of apathy and
despair, and in Deutero-Isaiah's time it was the prophet with a
message of hope who was suspect. Behind Deutero-Isaiah's oracles
one constantly discerns his urgent need to establish his credibility
and so to persuade his audience that Yahweh, who seemed to have
abandoned them, was at last preparing once more to act as their
redeemer.

The Exilic Situation

In order to form a clear idea of the way in which Deutero-Isaiah set
about proclaiming his message to a sceptical audience, it is necessary
to consider the circumstances in which he had to operate. Unfortu-

nately the evidence available about the manner of life of the Jewish exiles in Babylonia is extremely fragmentary. In view of the length of the period in question—about half a century—and of the fact that they were probably not all settled in the same area, and that local conditions as well as the policies of different reigns may have varied, there is a danger of over-generalization on an insufficient basis of evidence. However, although the exiles suffered from understandable feelings of depression and disillusionment (Ps. 137; Isa. 49:14), it is remarkable that they have left almost no record (Isa. 47:6, which is expressed in very general terms, is an exception) of harsh treatment. On the contrary, what information we have suggests that the exiles were able to resume something approaching normal life in their places of exile. The letter (Jer. 29) sent by Jeremiah to the first group of exiles of 597 B.C., who probably lived in the city of Babylon itself, advises them to reconcile themselves to Babylonian life and to 'build houses and live in them; plant gardens and eat their produce' (29:5). And on several occasions (e.g. Ezek. 8:1) Ezekiel speaks of his house, where he received 'the elders of Israel,' and where he uttered some of his prophecies. Whatever may be meant by the term 'elders' here, it clearly implies that the Jewish exiles had preserved or reinstituted some kind of social or administrative organisation among themselves.

These passages also imply that, at any rate in some places and at some times, the Jewish exiles were free to hold some sort of public gatherings or assemblies. That these included assemblies for public worship can be assumed. It can in any case be taken for granted that the Jewish faith did not stagnate during the exilic period. We know that this was in fact a crucially important period in its development, when it came to terms with the changed situation and eventually emerged with some newly acquired characteristics. We know also that there were many prophets at work among the exiles: not only Ezekiel and Deutero-Isaiah, but the prophets whom Jeremiah mentions in his letter, and doubtless others who succeeded them. The appearance of Deutero-Isaiah at the end of the period suggests a continuing prophetic tradition. The priesthood, too, survived: in the Book of Ezra there are lists of the priests and Levites and their families, descendants of those carried into exile in the deportations half a century earlier, who eventually returned to their homes.

It is inconceivable that Judaism could have survived for so long without some form of public worship. It is not possible to reconstruct this in detail, but it may be assumed that those who organized it will have made it as close as possible in character to the rites with which they had been familiar at the Jerusalem temple before its destruction, and will have made use of whatever liturgical material, oral or written, they had brought with them into exile.

Deutero-Isaiah's oracles are addressed not to individuals but to a whole community which calls itself Israel and Jacob, but can also be addressed as Jerusalem and as Zion. These titles reflect the exilic community's understanding of itself: they are Yahweh's chosen people Israel, but at the same time they regard themselves, even after so many years of exile, as citizens of Jerusalem, the holy city (48:2) which is their true home. These titles, which are used frequently and naturally by Deutero-Isaiah, only make sense if his oracles were addressed to assemblies, which identified themselves in some way with the whole people of Yahweh. Prophets must have audiences; and Deutero-Isaiah found his in such assemblies, whether gathered for worship or for some other purpose.

That Deutero-Isaiah, in his capacity as a prophet, should have played a part in the exiles' public worship is not *prima facie* improbable. Despite the well known condemnations of the public worship of their time by the prophets Hosea, Amos, Isaiah, Micah and Jeremiah it is now generally accepted that these prophets were not opposed to sacrificial worship *per se*, and that the contrast once made by earlier scholars between 'professional' cult-prophets and the classical prophets is not an absolute one. Public acts of worship may well have provided the setting for the utterances of some of the classical prophets in the pre-exilic period. Moreover, the worship of the Babylonian exiles probably did not include animal sacrifice, against which much of the invective of the earlier prophets had been directed. Other traditional modes of worship were available to them. Fortunately numerous examples of some of these, or of elements of them, have been preserved in the Book of Psalms: hymns or songs of praise to Yahweh, lamentations, songs of thanksgiving, priestly blessings, and also, to a lesser extent, oracles both of judgement and of salvation. Recent study has shown it to be very probable that much of this material originated well before the Exile. Its preservation suggests that it remained in regular use during the exilic period as well as in subsequent periods. A study of Deutero-Isaiah's oracles shows that he was familiar with, and made use of, most of these liturgical forms and also that he was familiar with many of the great religious and theological themes which are characteristic of the Psalms.

It is, however, improbable that all his oracles were spoken in situations of public worship. There were undoubtedly other opportunities of addressing assemblies of his fellow-exiles. In thus varying his methods and making use of opportunities of speaking wherever they presented themselves he was probably once more following in the steps of his pre-exilic predecessors, and also of Ezekiel earlier in the Exile who was visited in his home by 'certain of the elders of Israel' who came 'to enquire of Yahweh' and who thereupon pronounced an oracle (Ezek. 20:1). It was doubtless on such occasions outside the setting of worship that Deutero-Isaiah indulged in that type of reasoned argument expressed in his own words which is known as the 'disputation,' and in certain other kinds of speech which appear to have no liturgical connections.

Finally, what of the man himself? In the cases of almost all Deutero-Isaiah's predecessors something is revealed to us of their character and their reaction to their task, because it was impossible for an Israelite prophet to stand completely aloof from his message. His life and his mission were inextricably bound up together, and he was unable to escape the consequences of his words. This must be equally true of the—to us—anonymous prophet Deutero-Isaiah. Like that of Jeremiah before the fall of Jerusalem, his mission was an exceedingly dangerous one: it involved declaring in public, within the walls of the city of Babylon itself, that the city would shortly be conquered by a foreign enemy. Was he afraid of what the consequences of this subversive activity might be? Was he content to sacrifice himself in the cause of alerting his people to the good news? Or did he trust that Yahweh would protect him? Did he in fact suffer for his boldness? His oracles provide almost no information about either his character or his fate—unless we may take the picture of the Servant of Yahweh which appears in certain passages (42:1-4; 49:1-6; 50:4-9; 53) as a portrait of the prophet himself. But this question will be discussed in a later chapter.

Further Reading

There are considerable differences of opinion at the present time about the nature of Israelite prophecy and of the prophetical vocation. It is therefore recommended that *more than one* of the following works should be consulted.

*E.W. Heaton, *The Old Testament Prophets*, Harmondsworth: Penguin Books, 1958 / Atlanta: John Knox Press, rev. edition 1977

J. Lindblom, *Prophecy in Ancient Israel*, Oxford: Basil Blackwell, 1962, chapter 3

*G. von Rad, *The Message of the Prophets*, London: SCM Press, 1968 / New York: Harper and Row, 1972, chapters 1-5 (This is a revised version of material from G. von Rad, *Old Testament Theology*, Edinburgh and London: Oliver and Boyd, 1965, vol. II, Part One.)

*R.B.Y. Scott, *The Relevance of the Prophets*, New York and London: Macmillan, revised edition, 1968, chapters 1-5

C.F. Whitley, *The Prophetic Achievement*, Leiden: Brill, 1963

The following works presuppose some previous knowledge of the subject:

R.E. Clements, *Prophecy and Covenant* (Studies in Biblical Theology, 43), London: SCM Press, 1965, especially chapter 1

R.E. Clements, *Prophecy and Tradition* (Growing Points in Theology), Oxford: Basil Blackwell, 1975, especially chapter 3

The following works on the Babylonian Exile also offer somewhat different assessments of the period:

*P.R. Ackroyd, *Exile and Restoration. A Study of Hebrew Thought of the Sixth Century B.C.* (OTL), London: SCM Press / Philadelphia: Westminster Press, 1968, especially chapters 1-3, 8

Y. Kaufmann, *The Babylonian Captivity and Deutero-Isaiah*, New York: Union of American Hebrew Congregations, 1970, chapter 1

R.W. Klein, *Israel in Exile: A Theological Interpretation* (Overtures to Biblical Theology), Philadelphia: Fortress Press, 1979, especially chapters 1 and 5

*D.W. Thomas, 'The Sixth Century B.C.: A Creative Epoch in the History of Israel,' *Journal of Semitic Studies* 6 (1961) 33-46

C.F. Whitley, *The Exilic Age*, London: Longmans, 1957

4

THE ORACLES
AND THE BOOK

The mode of communication normally used by Israelite prophets was the spoken word. Only occasionally in the prophetical books is there a reference to a prophet's using writing to convey his message; and in such cases the message was usually very brief: a single word or phrase (Isa. 8:1; Jer. 22:30; Ezek. 24:2; 37:16, 20) or a single short oracle (Isa. 30:8; Hab. 2:2) or, in one case, a set of regulations (Ezek. 43:11). There is also one case of a prophet's sending a letter to a group of distant correspondents (Jer. 29). Only when there was a special reason did a prophet write his message down. In the Book of Jeremiah there are indeed references to the recording of the prophet's main message in writing (Jer. 30:2; 36; 45:1; 51:60), but these were records of oracles which had already been communicated verbally. There is no direct evidence of a prophet's using the written word as his primary means of communication: when the means of communication is specified it is, except for the few cases already mentioned, that of direct speech: 'Go and say' (Isa. 6:9; 22:15); 'Isaiah . . . came . . . and said' (Isa. 38:1; 39:3); 'Go and proclaim in the hearing of Jerusalem' (Jer. 2:2); 'Stand in the gate . . . and proclaim there this word, saying . . . ' (Jer. 7:2); 'And you shall speak my words to them' (Ezek. 2:7).

This does not mean that prophets never played any part in the process by which their oracles were subsequently recorded in writing and gradually formed into the prophetic books which we now possess. If the passages in the Book of Jeremiah referred to above are to be believed, it was Jeremiah himself who caused the first collection of his oracles to be committed to writing; and this may well have been the case with some other prophets. But there is a great difference between a written collection of speeches delivered on a variety of occasions before live audiences and a single literary work, or even a series of long poems, composed from the beginning for a reading public.

A Literary Unity?

In the case of Deutero-Isaiah no direct statements are available to us about the manner or circumstances in which his message was originally communicated to his audience. The evidence must be sought in the character and form of the oracles themselves. We must ask whether the book (i.e., chapters 40-55) appears to have a single coherent plan and continuity of theme, or whether in form and subject-matter it gives the impression of having been composed from a number of separate parts, each complete in itself; and, if the latter is the case, whether these are themselves fairly long literary compositions or short units comparable with the oral utterances of earlier prophets. In view of the long tradition of oral utterance which Deutero-Isaiah inherited as a prophet, the burden of proof lies with those who believe that he broke away from that tradition to adopt the style, methods and techniques of a writer.

One of the most elaborate defences of the literary theory was that of Muilenburg, who held that 'the poems of Second Isaiah . . . are so elaborate in their composition and in the detail of technical devices that they must have been written rather than spoken' (Muilenburg, 386). He argued that chapters 40-55 consist of twenty-one poems by the same author, each having its own distinct theme and each divided into a number of carefully formed strophes. Although the whole collection is dominated by a single theological standpoint, the distinctiveness of each poem as a separate literary creation is shown not only by its thematic unity but also by its inner literary structure: a rich and varied use of stylistic and rhetorical devices such as assonance, imagery, contrast, repetition, wordplay and recapitulation has moulded it into a literary masterpiece complete in itself.

No one has made a greater contribution than Muilenburg to the appreciation of the qualities of Deutero-Isaiah's poetry. However, three objections may be made to his view that he was essentially a writer. First, recent study of 'oral poetry,' a phenomenon found among many peoples, throws doubt on Muilenburg's assertion that only written poetry can manifest such subtlety of composition. Secondly, in his discovery of stylistic patterns Muilenburg appears to many readers of Deutero-Isaiah to have been himself over-subtle, seeing significance in features which may not have been perceived as such by their author, and finding patterns and structures which are not apparent to a detached observer. Thirdly, Muilenburg too readily

dismissed the conclusions of the form-critics, who have identified in
Deutero-Isaiah's prophecies a large number of originally independent,
fairly short, oracles, each having a clearly defined form and a distinct
function in the carrying out of his prophetic ministry. Muilenburg
held that Deutero-Isaiah in composing his long poems used stylistic
elements from these traditional forms only for a literary purpose: for
him they had totally lost their original functions. This interpretation
isolates Deutero-Isaiah from effective participation in the everyday
religious life of the Babylonian exiles and makes of him rather an
observer: a poet and a writer. If this is so he can be called a prophet
only in a new and special sense. But this view is unwarranted:
Deutero-Isaiah's oracles as delineated by the form-critics make excel-
lent sense in the context of that religious life. That Deutero-Isaiah
was a superb poet must and should be acknowledged; but he was first
and foremost a prophet, who continued to use, though often with
considerable originality, the methods and speech-forms which he had
inherited from the past.

Form Criticism

In order to substantiate the above remarks it is first necessary to
enquire into the nature of form criticism and to ask how it has
contributed to the study of Deutero-Isaiah. Form criticism (in German
Formgeschichte, 'form *history*,' is the corresponding term) is a method
of studying traditional forms of speech—that is, speech or writing
which is conventional in character. In modern times such forms may
consist of single phrases like 'How do you do?' or 'Good luck!,' or of
more elaborate compositions such as letters, with their relatively
fixed elements of sender's address, date, formula of greeting ('Dear
X'), main section, concluding formula (e.g. 'Yours ever') and signature.
It was the contention of Gunkel, who first applied this method to the
Old Testament especially in his studies of the narratives in the Book
of Genesis and of the Psalms, that such conventional forms of speech,
which in the conservative societies of the ancient Near East exercised
a much more powerful and pervasive influence as models of speech
than they do today, were developed as responses to certain regularly
occurring situations, particularly situations of crisis, in the life of a
community or of an individual (the *Sitz im Leben*). Each of the
various types of speech unmistakably reflected one such typical situation; and only when it was recognized that this was so could the

extant examples of it in the Old Testament be properly understood.

The application of form criticism to the prophetical books was initiated by Gunkel himself and carried further by other scholars. It was first applied to Deutero-Isaiah by Gressmann, and pursued with increasing refinement by others, especially Köhler, Mowinckel (1931), Elliger, Begrich (1938), von Waldow (1953) and Westermann (1964). More recent contributions have been made by Schoors, Melugin and Merendino.

Form criticism, when used sensitively, is capable of furthering the study of the prophetical books in a number of ways. Firstly, the study of the essential features and structure of the various types of prophetic speech makes it possible to identify examples of these within a particular book. If it can be established where these oracles begin and end, the first step has been taken towards the identification of the component elements of the book and so towards an understanding of the process by which it reached its present form.

Secondly, the study of the typical structure and phraseology of a particular type of oracle on the basis of all the extant examples found throughout the prophetical books may make it possible to understand more clearly than before the precise role and mode of operation of the Israelite prophet. For example, in a passage like Isa. 49:14-23, which is obviously intended to bring to its hearers a message of hope, the reference (verse 14) to an earlier lament closely resembling certain lamentations in the Book of Psalms suggests that such oracles of salvation formed part of a liturgical sequence in which, it was believed, Yahweh, through his appointed representative, replied, in this case positively, to the people's cry of despair.

Thirdly—and here the German word *Formgeschichte* has its point— the study of a particular type of oracle as it occurs in the various prophetical books may reveal a historical development or modification of its form and content which in turn points to a theological development or even to a change in the circumstances or the character of prophecy itself. This aspect of form criticism is particularly important in the case of Deutero-Isaiah, since it has shown that he treated the traditional forms with unusual freedom. In this way the path is cleared for an understanding of the special characteristics of a prophet's theology, which would otherwise be partly obscured if—as in the case of Deutero-Isaiah—the text as it stands presents itself as an undifferentiated mass of somewhat repetitive theological statements.

Form criticism, then, is an extremely useful instrument for studying the prophetical literature. However, it has its limitations and dangers. Firstly, it can only be usefully applied to speech or writing which is mainly conventional in character. With regard to more original speech or writing it may help to distinguish conventional elements from what is completely original; but in so far as an author breaks free from convention and expresses his thoughts freely in his own way, form-critical analysis as defined above is clearly inapplicable. In Deutero-Isaiah there are certainly passages of this kind.

Secondly, form criticism can be carried to excess. The enthusiastic form-critic sometimes falls into the trap of 'discovering' conventional speech-forms where none exists. This is particularly so where a prophet is supposed to have borrowed alien speech-forms: that is, speech-forms which originally belonged to other spheres of life than prophecy. That prophets sometimes did this in order to emphasize a point is undeniable. Amos imitated the form of the dirge (Amos 5:1-2) and Isaiah that of the love song (Isa. 5:1-2). It has been supposed that in Isa. 55:1 Deutero-Isaiah borrowed the traditional cry of the water-seller (though according to other scholars this is the language of the wisdom tradition!). There is, of course, a sense in which all speech is conventional, since it is composed of words and phrases in common use. The problem is to decide in each case whether, in using language which is reminiscent of the specialised language of some other sphere of life, a prophet was deliberately evoking particular associations or not. To docket every phrase in a kind of form-critical filing cabinet would be an absurd misuse of form criticism which would reveal an insensitivity to a prophet's spontaneity and creative imagination.

Form criticism can also be carried to excess by an over-minute sub-classification of prophetic types of speech. Thus Westermann in his study of the speech-forms of Deutero-Isaiah subdivides the 'oracles of salvation' into two distinct types to which he attributes different origins and *Sitz im Leben*: the 'promise of salvation' (*Heilszusage*) and the 'announcement of salvation' (*Heilsankündigung*). The difference between the two may however have a simpler explanation. The *Heilsankündigung* may simply be a more loosely constructed equivalent of the more traditional *Heilszusage*—an example of Deutero-Isaiah's tendency to free himself from conventional forms of speech.

Finally it is important to realize that a prophet may sometimes use conventional forms of speech for rhetorical purposes, separating them from their original setting and giving them a new function. This phenomenon was already recognized by Gunkel outside the prophetical literature, and was given prominence by him in his study of the Psalms. It is one of the aspects of the study of the *history* of forms, and has already been referred to. In the case of Deutero-Isaiah it has been argued above that his oracles include many of a traditional kind which were not simply literary elements in longer poems but were 'live' spoken messages from Yahweh to an assembled people. But this did not prevent him from borrowing, as had his predecessors, 'alien' forms on other occasions to reinforce his message. Isa. 55:1 has already been mentioned as a possible example of this. But he also borrowed on a larger scale: for example, in some passages he depicted an imaginary scene in a court of law, using a legal setting and terminology in order to present his argument in a striking way. In such cases, where the original function of a form of speech has been lost in a new context, form criticism can assist by identifying the original *Sitz im Leben*, but beyond thus noting a new stage in the history of the form in question it can throw little light on the interpretation of the passages concerned. As has been pointed out by Fohrer, the change of function means that the key to their interpretation must now be sought not in the origin of the forms employed but in the new contexts and in the particular way in which the prophet has adapted them to his own purpose. In this process of interpretation form criticism has no part to play.

The Oracle of Salvation

It has already been suggested above that some of Deutero-Isaiah's oracles may have been spoken in the setting of meetings for public worship, which would have provided him with an opportunity for a hearing. This hypothesis is particularly convincing in the case of the type of oracle known as the *oracle of salvation* (*Heilsorakel* or *Heilswort*).

It was Gunkel who first put forward the theory that the individual lamentation in the Book of Psalms and some other Old Testament books had as its *Sitz im Leben* a rite in which persons in distress made their appeal to Yahweh at the sanctuary. He further suggested that this recital might have been followed by an oracle, spoken by a priest, giving them the assurance that their prayer had been heard. This hypothesis was further developed by Küchler, Mowinckel and

Begrich. The fact that no actual example of such an 'oracle of salvation' appended to a lamentation has been preserved in the Book of Psalms is simply explained: the oracle, unlike the lamentation, was not a completely fixed form of words, but was composed *ad lib.*: it was Yahweh's prerogative to give or to withhold an oracle, and to determine on each occasion what its contents should be. Only the fixed part of the liturgy was preserved for common use. The priest who pronounced the oracle was regarded as Yahweh's mouthpiece.

Despite the lack of concrete evidence in the form of an extant oracle preserved together with its corresponding lamentation, this hypothesis seemed to be the most plausible explanation of certain phenomena: in particular, it explained the change of mood on the part of the worshipper which occurs in some psalms (e.g. Ps. 22:22) suddenly and without any apparent explanation, from one of dejection and self-pity to one of joy and certainty that his petition had been heard and approved. This change, it was argued, was caused by the intervention of an oracle of salvation which had originally divided the psalm into two parts, of which the second was recited after the oracle had been spoken.

A further step was taken with the suggestion, first made in Gunkel's *Einleitung in die Psalmen* (1933, 246) which Begrich completed after Gunkel's death, that examples of the oracle of salvation are to be found in the Old Testament, particularly in Deutero-Isaiah. These are, however, not attached to any lamentation psalms but stand entirely by themselves. Begrich developed this theory in later studies. He argued (1938) that Deutero-Isaiah must have been familiar with the lamentation rite and borrowed the genre of the oracle of salvation from it as an 'alien form' for a purely rhetorical purpose: as an effective means of conveying his message of salvation to the exiles.

Further study, especially by von Waldow (1953), went further still. Von Waldow suggested that Begrich's view that Deutero-Isaiah's use of the oracle of salvation was no more than a literary imitation detached from its original setting did not take account of the evidence provided by the text of Deutero-Isaiah itself. He observed that some of his oracles of salvation contain phrases which point to an actual cultic setting: their initial words look like quotations of phrases, or even whole sections, taken from lamentations which had actually been recited by the exiles at their meetings for worship. In other words, Deutero-Isaiah had picked up these self-pitying epithets and appeals for help, and, speaking in the name of Yahweh, had assured the petitioners that their situation was now to be radically transformed. Thus 49:14 makes a specific reference to the recital of such a lamentation: 'But Zion has said, "Yahweh has forsaken me, my Lord has forgotten me".' 51:9-10 similarly is a quotation from such a lamentation, reminding Yahweh of his great deeds in the past and appealing for a further display of his power now. In other examples the prophet, in addressing his audience, picked up phrases which they had evidently applied to themselves in describing their state of distress: 'you worm Jacob' (41:14); 'you whose heart fails [following a probable emendation], who are far from deliverance' (46:12); 'to one deeply despised' (49:7); 'you who have drunk from Yahweh's hand the cup of his wrath' (51:17); 'O barren one, who did not bear' (54:1); 'O afflicted one, storm-tossed and not comforted' (54:11). Much of this language is closely paralleled in lamentations preserved in the Book of Psalms, and is at the same time peculiarly appropriate to the situation of the exiles. Indeed it has strong affinities with the language of the lamentations in the Book of Lamentations, which are themselves lamentations of the people from the exilic period (in Palestine, not Babylonia). Unlike earlier oracles of salvation, these examples in Deutero-Isaiah have been preserved because of their authorship: they form part of the collected oracles of the prophet Deutero-Isaiah.

The above interpretation is due primarily to the researches of von Waldow. Gunkel had postulated the existence of the oracle of salvation and suggested that some examples might be found in Deutero-Isaiah; Begrich identified these examples and analysed their form, but thought that they were literary imitations; finally von Waldow argued for a genuine cultic setting for them.

In the working out of his theory, however, von Waldow was faced with a dual problem: whilst the oracles of salvation postulated by Gunkel and Begrich were *priestly* oracles pronounced in reply to the lamentation of an *individual*, Deutero-Isaiah's oracles of salvation, although some of them were couched in individual terms, were *prophetic* oracles, and were given in reply to the *corporate* lamentations of a community gathered for worship.

The first of these differences, that between an individual and a corporate *Sitz im Leben*, does not present a very serious problem. Certain texts in other Old Testament books—e.g. Joel 2:17-19—attest the use of the oracle of salvation in reply to the corporate lamentation. Moreover corporate lamentations were sometimes expressed in individual terms, with the community personified as an individual (as in Lam. 1 and 3). Isa. 49:14 is a quotation from such a lamentation, in which the community of the exiles is personified as a woman, 'Zion,' and which is appropriately answered in an oracle of salvation couched in similar terms.

The problem of prophetic as against priestly oracle is a more serious one. The question is whether Gunkel's and Begrich's assumption that the oracle of salvation had always in the past been spoken by a priest is correct. Von Waldow, utilizing more recent researches on the relationship between prophets and the cult, argued that cultic prophets as well as priests had been entrusted with the pronouncement of such oracles, and that Deutero-Isaiah was thus reviving an older practice. Westermann, like Begrich, regarded all Deutero-Isaiah's oracles as unrelated to the exilic cult. But in discussing the original *Sitz im Leben* of Deutero-Isaiah's oracles of salvation (*Heilswort*) he made a new distinction. Deutero-Isaiah had, for his own purposes, borrowed two quite distinct types of oracle. The first, the 'promise of salvation' (*Heilszusage*) was originally the *priestly* reply to the individual lamentation, and proclaimed Yahweh's decision and action as if it were already an accomplished fact. The second, the 'announcement of salvation' (*Heilsankündigung*) had a typically *prophetic* function, the prediction of Yahweh's action in the future. It is the latter, according to Westermann, which begins with a quotation from a previous lamentation; but in spite of this fact it is not to be seen as a cultic oracle replying to the lamentation, but as a kind of reflection on it, presented outside the cult as a prophetic word. The type of lamentation from which it takes its start is the corporate lamentation, and this also marks it out as distinct from the 'promise of salvation.'

According to Westermann the promises of salvation in Deutero-Isaiah are not numerous, and almost all occur within chapters 41-44. They comprise 41:8-13; 41:14-16; 43:1-4; 43:5-7; 44:1-5 and perhaps 54:4-6. They follow, in general, a strict pattern whose cultic origins are shown by their similarity to examples of Babylonian oracles addressed by priests to kings in answer to their prayers. The announcement of salvation has a much looser structure. Again there are only a few clear examples of it: 41:17-20; 42:14-17; 43:16-21; 45:14-17; 49:7-12. There are, however, many other passages in Deutero-Isaiah which announce salvation to the exiles but have no fixed form. In these there is a tendency for other speech-forms to be used in conjunction with the message of salvation proper, resulting in mixed forms which cannot be analysed form-critically.

Westermann is undoubtedly correct in his agreement with earlier scholars that the first of these types of oracle displays a form which corresponds perfectly to what is to be expected from a cultic oracle of salvation. His analysis of the *promise of salvation* may best be illustrated from 41:14-16:

1. *The address*: 'You worm Jacob, you louse [this is a probable emendation] Israel' (14a). Compare 41:8, 9; 43:1a; 44:1. The address is missing in 43:5-7 and 54:4-6.

2. *The assurance of salvation*: 'Fear not!' (14a). This phrase, which occurs in all the promises of salvation (also in 41:10; 43:1; 43:5; 44:2b; 54:4) is in itself an assurance that the petitioner's prayer will be answered, since it is spoken as Yahweh's own authoritative word. It may occur either at the beginning of the address or immediately after it.

3. *The basis of the assurance*: (a) '"I will help you," says Yahweh'; (b) 'the Holy One of Israel is your Redeemer' (14b). Here Yahweh substantiates his word of assurance, answering the appeals for help by affirming his presence, his intimate relationship with the petitioners, and the fact that he is already taking steps to help them. In four cases (here and 43:1; 43:5; 54:4) this section is introduced by the explanatory particle *kî*, 'For.' It may consist of one or both of two elements: a statement about Yahweh's relationship to the petitioner (here 'the Holy One of Israel is your Redeemer'; elsewhere 'For I am with you,' 41:10; 43:5; 'You are mine,' 43:1; 'For your Maker . . . is your Redeemer,' 54:5) and a statement in the perfect tense (indicating certainty) that Yahweh is about to help and is already helping (here 'I will help you'; elsewhere 'I will strengthen you . . . ,' 41:10b; 'I will redeem you . . . ,' 43:1b). This section is lacking in 44:1-5.

4. *The consequences of Yahweh's action*, expressed more concretely and in greater detail, mainly in future (imperfect) tenses: verses 15-16a. Compare 41:11, 12; 43:2; 43:5-6; 44:3-5; 54:4.

5. *Yahweh's ultimate purpose*: verse 16b. This can be seen clearly only in two of the other oracles: 43:7; 44:5.

It is more difficult to agree with Westermann and his followers about his second category of oracles of salvation, the so-called *announcement of salvation*. Westermann analysed this category in the following way:

1. Allusion to a previous lamentation
2. Announcement of salvation
        a. God's turning to his people
        b. God's intervention
3. God's ultimate purpose

There is in the first place considerable difference of opinion about the number of passages which conform to this pattern. Schoors, for example, added nine more (46:12-13; 49:14-26; 51:1-3+6; 51:7-8; 51:9-14; 51:17-23; 54:7-10; 54:11-17; 55:1-3) to Westermann's five, and omitted one of Westermann's (45:14-17).

In almost every respect the attempt to find a common structure in these passages fails to convince: some, but not all, of them have an introductory section not mentioned by Westermann; the allusions to a preceding lamentation are not always clear; the attempt to distinguish between God's 'turning to his people' and God's 'intervention' frequently seems artificial; and the final section is often lacking. The form-critical method seems to fail badly in dealing with these passages. Many of them can be identified as distinct units on the basis of such literary criteria as obvious opening and concluding phrases, change of style and the introduction of a new *mise en scène*, but not on the grounds of conformity to a set pattern. The question of their use in the cult cannot therefore be answered, except in cases where the allusion to a previous lamentation is clear, as for example in 49:14. In these cases, in view of Deutero-Isaiah's tendency to break away from the old forms and to try out new ones, there is ground for supposing that they are cultic oracles of a freer type, spoken, like those which have a stricter form, as oracles of salvation in answer to those lamentations. Whether this is true of all passages which proclaim the imminence of Yahweh's salvation to the exiles cannot be determined.

The Hymn

One important feature of Israel's worship in the days when the Temple at Jerusalem was still in use was the *Hymn*, or psalm of praise, in which the assembled people, no doubt especially at the major festivals of the year, offered their praise to Yahweh. Some of these hymns are quite elaborate; but basically their structure was very simple, consisting of only two parts: first, a summons to praise Yahweh, usually expressed in the imperative mood but sometimes in the cohortative ('Let us . . . '), and addressed sometimes to Israel alone but sometimes to the peoples of the world, or even to the whole created universe; and secondly a statement about Yahweh's benevolence towards his people or about the consequences of that benevolence—his great deeds performed in the past, in creation or in history. This section, the main section of the hymn, is often introduced by the word *kî*, 'For,' since it states the reason why praise should be offered. This simple structure is well illustrated by Psalm 117, the shortest and most compact of the hymns in the Book of Psalms:

> Praise Yahweh, all nations!
> Extol him, all peoples!
> For great is his steadfast love towards us;
> and the faithfulness of Yahweh endures for ever.

The style of Deutero-Isaiah, as we shall see, was greatly influenced throughout by that of these liturgical hymns. But more than that: there are several passages among his oracles which are complete hymns in themselves, having exactly the same structure and theme as that of the hymns in the Book of Psalms. Three of the clearest examples are 42:10-13; 44:23; 49:13. The last two of these are sufficiently short to be quoted in full:

> Sing, O heavens, for Yahweh has done it;
> shout, O depths of the earth;
> break forth into singing, O mountains,
> O forest, and every tree in it!
> For Yahweh has redeemed Jacob,
> and will be glorified in Israel.

> Sing for joy, O heavens, and exult, O earth;
> break forth, O mountains, into singing!
> For Yahweh has comforted his people,
> and has compassion for his afflicted.

Westermann, using a phrase borrowed from Gunkel, called these hymns of Deutero-Isaiah's 'eschatological psalms of praise.' He regarded them as a special category of 'psalms of praise' (he does not use the word 'hymn') on the grounds of their form as well as of their function: according to him it is only in these psalms (of which a few are to be found in other prophetical books) that the summons to worship is followed by a statement about Yahweh's actions rather than about his personal qualities (as in Ps. 117). The summons to worship normally belongs to what he calls the 'descriptive psalm of praise' and the statement about Yahweh's actions to the 'declarative psalm of praise.' The 'eschatological psalm of praise' was a form possibly invented by Deutero-Isaiah himself, and is characteristically prophetic in character. Westermann's form-critical analysis seems here to be over-subtle. There is really little difference between psalms like Ps. 117 and the two psalms of Deutero-Isaiah quoted above. When in psalms like Ps. 117 Yahweh is praised for his personal qualities, these—as Westermann himself admits—are not abstract virtues but concrete attitudes of Yahweh directly related to, and indeed generative of, his specific attitudes towards Israel: the two sets of psalm are really referring to the same thing. In fact these psalms of Deutero-Isaiah, if they had found their way into the Book of Psalms, would not appear in any way strange. Moreover the combination of summons to praise and statement about Yahweh's concrete actions in history is found already in what Westermann himself admits to be one of the oldest hymns in the Old Testament, the Song of Miriam in Exod. 15:21 (placed by Westermann in the sub-category of 'songs of victory'):

> Sing to Yahweh, for he has triumphed gloriously;
> the horse and its rider he has thrown into the sea.

However, Westermann's designation of these hymns of Deutero-Isaiah as 'eschatological psalms of praise,' though a somewhat unfortunate one because it begs the questions what is meant by 'eschatology' and whether Deutero-Isaiah's message can properly be called eschatological, rightly draws attention to their unique *function* in the context of Deutero-Isaiah's oracles. It is unlikely that they are simply hymns which he was commissioned to compose for the public worship of the Babylonian exiles, since it is clear from his other oracles that their mood was hardly one in which they would wish to sing new hymns in praise of Yahweh, who, they thought, had forgotten them. Rather they are to be thought of as simply part of Deutero-Isaiah's message: in fact one passage which has the form of a hymn (52:9-10) is actually embedded in a longer oracle. Deutero-Isaiah used the form of the hymn in order to impress upon his audience his conviction that Yahweh's intervention to help them was both certain and imminent. The perfect tense which always appears in these hymns with Yahweh as the subject (e.g. 'Yahweh has comforted his people'), which had previously been used in the psalms (specifically in the corporate thanksgiving psalms, but see also once more Exod. 15:21) to refer to his actions in the past, is now used by

Deutero-Isaiah as a 'prophetic perfect' or 'perfect of certainty' indicating a future action in the making: redemption is so near that it can
be regarded as actually achieved.

In addition to this little group of complete hymns, there are many
phrases and stylistic devices in Deutero-Isaiah's oracles which are
clearly based on the style of the hymn. The most striking examples of
this are the passages (e.g. 42:5; 43:1; 43:16-17; 44:2; 45:18) in which
he describes the nature and activity, especially the creative activity,
of Yahweh in a series of participial clauses (usually rendered in
English translations by 'who . . . '). A good example of this style is
42:5:

> Thus says God, Yahweh,
>> who created the heavens and stretched them out,
>> who spread forth the earth and what grows from it,
> who gives breath to the people on it
> and spirit to those who walk on it . . .

In the Book of Psalms this style is represented by passages such as
Ps. 103:3-5; 104:1-4; 136:4-7; 147:8-9, 14-17. A particularly good
basis for comparison is provided by Ps. 104:1-4:

> Bless Yahweh, O my soul! . . .
>> who coverest thyself with light as with a garment,
> who hast stretched out the heavens like a tent,
>> who hast laid the beams of thy chambers on the waters,
> who makest the clouds thy chariot,
>> who ridest on the wings of the wind,
> who makest the winds thy messengers,
>> fire and flame thy ministers.

It is to be noted that in the hymns in the Book of Psalms such
passages are always attached to the summons to worship ('Praise/Bless
Yahweh . . . ' or some equivalent phrase) and form part of the main
section of the hymn. In the examples in Deutero-Isaiah, however,
they have become part of the prophetic message, and almost always
follow the 'messenger formula' 'Thus says Yahweh.' Here also their
function is to evoke those sentiments of awe and dependence on
Yahweh as the creator of the world and creator and sustainer of
Israel of which the cultic hymns had been the expression and which
the exiles were in danger of losing, but which were indispensable if

they were to be convinced by the promise of help which was to follow
in the ensuing oracle of salvation.

Sometimes such descriptions of Yahweh's nature and activity are
placed in the mouth of Yahweh himself, so that he is represented as
praising himself, as in 46:9-10:

> ... for I am God, and there is no other;
>   I am God, and there is none like me,
> declaring the end from the beginning
>   and from ancient times things not yet done,
> saying, 'My counsel shall stand,
>   and I will accomplish all my purpose . . . .'

Other passages in which Yahweh praises himself include 41:4b;
42:8; 43:10-13; 44:24-28; 45:6-7; 48:12-13; 51:15. It has been argued
that in such passages, which are unparalleled in the Old Testament,
Deutero-Isaiah was influenced by the style of the 'hymns of self-
praise' used in the Babylonian cult, in which various deities, speaking
in the first person, proclaim their powers and virtues; but this can
only remain a possible hypothesis. What is clear is that Deutero-
Isaiah was deeply imbued with both the language and the spirit of the
hymnic tradition of Israel, and used it frequently and in various
ways, including the direct address of Yahweh to his people which was
the principal mode of prophetic speech, to express and drive home
his message to the exiles.

The Trial Scene

Deutero-Isaiah's message was essentially a simple one, and he expressed
it mainly by means of the various oracles of salvation, in which
Yahweh spoke through him. But his task did not end there. He had to
deal with an audience which was reluctant to accept his message as
authentic. Consequently he was obliged to take on the role of Yahweh's
advocate, attempting to substantiate his central message by means of
argument. Such arguments are to be found in what Schoors calls 'the
polemical genres' in the book: forms of speech to which different
scholars have given various names, of which perhaps the most appropriate are the *'trial scene'* (*Gerichtsszene*) and the *'disputation'* (*Dispu-
tationswort*). Their *Sitz im Leben* is unlikely to have been that of

public worship; the atmosphere is more like that of a debate or a dispute. These are really no more than literary devices or ways of expressing an argument in what Deutero-Isaiah intended to be a vivid and convincing manner. In fact neither conforms to a rigid pattern, and it is not always possible to distinguish the one from the other. Moreover in both types of speech Deutero-Isaiah, in his desire to use every possible device to make his point, has pressed into service motifs from quite different spheres, such as the hymn, the divine self-praise and the oracle of salvation. It is therefore not surprising that there are considerable differences of opinion among scholars about the identification of these two forms of speech.

The device of the *trial scene* had been used by earlier prophets (e.g. Isa. 3:13-15; Micah 6:1-5) to give additional effectiveness to their oracles of *judgement against Israel* by placing them in the fictitious setting of a court of law. This device is probably based on the ordinary legal procedures in use in pre-exilic Israel, which consisted of a summons issued to the accuser and the defendant, an invitation to the parties to state their cases, speeches by the two parties and sometimes by the witnesses, the judgement and the sentence. The account of the trial of Jeremiah (Jer. 26) illustrates most of these features.

Very few, if any, of the trial scenes in Deutero-Isaiah or in the pre-exilic prophets include all the features of an actual trial. The only criterion which can be applied for their identification is that a passage should include a sufficient number of these features to make it recognizable as a trial scene.

In Deutero-Isaiah's oracles there are a few traces of the earlier use of the trial-scene to express the divine judgement against Israel. Not surprisingly, these do not amount to a full scale condemnation: there is in Deutero-Isaiah no oracle of judgement on Israel in the full sense of the word. Israel's past sin is acknowledged and treated with full seriousness, but the threatened judgement has now fallen, and the time for forgiveness and restoration has arrived (40:2; 50:1-3).

The oracle of judgement had normally consisted of two principal elements: the indictment of Israel and the announcement of the sentence, both pronounced by Yahweh as both accuser and judge (e.g. Amos 4:1-3). The only echo of this in Deutero-Isaiah's oracles occurs in 43:22-28; but the purpose for which it is used is quite different from the original purpose of the oracle of judgement, and is typical of

Deutero-Isaiah's inventive mind: the indictment is first solemnly pronounced as if yet another terrible disaster is about to be announced; but then in verse 25, instead of the expected judicial sentence, there occurs an incredible word of grace and forgiveness: 'I, I am he who blots out your transgressions for my own sake, and I will not remember your sins'! In this amazing volte-face we have the essence of Deutero-Isaiah's message in a nutshell: the exiles must not forget that their punishment was fully deserved; but they must also learn that the just God is also a God of infinite grace.

Westermann identified two other passages, 42:18-25 and 50:1-3, as having some features of the oracle of judgement against Israel; but the evidence for this is less convincing. In any case these passages are certainly not in any sense complete examples of the trial scene. The only other chapter in which echoes of judgement on Israel occur is chapter 48, where there is a strange alternation of promise and accusation. But here Westermann has shown convincingly that the latter element is not part of the original message of Deutero-Isaiah: this is one of the very few examples of editorial addition to the original, the work of an editor whose intention was to adapt the teaching of Deutero-Isaiah for a later generation which seemed to him to deserve further castigation.

Deutero-Isaiah used the form of the trial scene mainly for quite a different purpose: *to demonstrate the worthlessness of the gods worshipped by the other nations*. The 'trial' here seems to be not so much a criminal trial as a 'fact-finding' enquiry. Yahweh's opponents are the foreign nations and their gods; and the question at issue is, 'Who is the true God?' As will be seen in Chapter 5, this is one of Deutero-Isaiah's most characteristic types of argument.

There are at least five clear examples of this kind of trial scene: 41:1-5; 41:21-29; 43:8-13; 44:6-8+21-22 (verses 9-20 have been interpolated); 45:20-25. There are also other passages in which some of these motifs appear.

41:21-29 may be taken as a model in which a number of the constitutive elements appear. The language of verse 21, which sets the scene, is clearly that of the law court. Yahweh is the presiding judge, though he is also one of the parties in dispute, a feature which will be considered below. The other side consists of the pagan gods. These are addressed and asked to present proofs of their activity and thus effectively of their existence. Verses 22-23 state the nature of the matter in dispute and the kind of evidence to be admitted. But the gods are shown by their silence to be non-existent. Yahweh then presents his own case, which is the main reason for the use of the device of the trial scene (verses 25-28) and reaches his conclusion. The concluding judgement in verse 29 is that the other so-called gods have no existence. A similar pattern but with slightly different features is followed in the other examples. 41:1 gives a fuller account of the setting. 43:9-12 mentions the witnesses: the nations on one side, Israel on the other. 44:6-8+21-22 ends somewhat differently from the others, with a divine promise to Israel (verse 22). But all these trial scenes are intended to leave the exiles with the impression that Yahweh is firmly in charge of events.

Most form-critics who have given attention to the matter (e.g. Köhler, Begrich, Boecker) have supposed that the trial speech in the prophetical books is a literary imitation of normal court procedure: that is, of the 'judgement in the gate' of the city, where all the adult male citizens were eligible to form the court. The procedure was very simple, and there was no professional judge. This would explain the curious fact that in these prophetic scenes Yahweh was at the same time a party to the dispute and also the one who passed judgement. Some scholars, however, have felt that this is an inadequate explanation and have offered alternative models for these scenes. Harvey, for example, argued that the model was a very special kind of trial: that held by the suzerain or great king to judge a vassal who had broken the conditions of the international treaty by which he was bound. In such a case the suzerain was the aggrieved party but also the judge who pronounced sentence. There are no clear references to this procedure in the Old Testament, but examples of something of the kind are to be found elsewhere in the ancient Near East, and in the immediate pre-exilic period kings of Judah who were vassals of Assyria or Babylon might well have been subjected to it. Alternatively it has been suggested (by Würthwein and von Waldow) that the model for some at least of the prophetical scenes of judgement against Israel may have been a 'cultic lawsuit' in which Yahweh, represented by the priests, judged Israel as their suzerain for the breach of his covenant. Such a suggestion, however, is speculative. Scholarly discussion of this problem still continues.

The Disputation

The *disputation* is a form of argument in which the speaker is usually not Yahweh but the prophet. This form is not entirely lacking in the recorded words of the earlier prophets, but in Deutero-Isaiah it is more frequent and more fully developed. It has been suggested that this form of speech has been borrowed from the wisdom tradition: in particular, that it is the kind of argument which might have taken place in 'wisdom schools.' But there is no evidence that such disputations ever took place in such a setting. In fact the forms of argument used by Deutero-Isaiah in his role of persuader are common to all rational speech.

Westermann pointed out that Deutero-Isaiah had a predilection for one kind of argument in particular: the argument which proceeds by analogy. The speaker begins by stating a fact about which his audience would be in agreement: a self-evident fact which either is a matter of common sense or forms part of the common religious traditions of Israel which no one would dispute. From this he proceeds, by means of analogy, to state a proposition which his audience had not previously been prepared to accept.

So in 40:12-17 and 40:18-26 the prophet argues from the Israelite belief that Yahweh is the creator of the world to the proposition that he must therefore be the one who controls historical persons and events. In 40:27-31 he argues from Yahweh's almightiness to the proposition that he can make available to the weary and dispirited exiles all the strength which they need. In 45:9-13 he argues from the common-sense proposition that it is absurd for a created object like a pot to criticise the potter who made it, or for a foetus to question its parents, to the proposition that it is equally nonsensical for Israel to question Yahweh, their maker, about his plans. And in 55:8-11 he argues from the regularity and inevitability of the fertilising power of the rain sent from heaven by Yahweh to the proposition that Yahweh's word spoken by the prophets equally cannot fail to achieve the purpose for which it was sent. Deutero-Isaiah was not, however, restricted to this kind of argument, but used others as well; and there are other passages such as 46:9-11; 48:1-11; 48:12-16 which are also best classified as disputations although their arguments proceed on other lines.

Other Forms of Speech

The above are the principal forms of speech used by Deutero-Isaiah. It should be noted that some passages do not come under any of these headings, either because they have composite forms with elements belonging to more than one type, or because they belong to no recognised type but bear the marks of Deutero-Isaiah's original mind. Various motifs drawn from yet other forms of speech occur sporadically throughout the oracles, but these are mainly quite short and not in themselves of major importance as vehicles of Deutero-Isaiah's message. References to them will be found in the commentaries. There is however one passage which ought to be mentioned here. Chapter 47 is a single poem of unusual length, and is the only example of its kind in Deutero-Isaiah. It belongs to a type which occurs fairly frequently in other prophetical books: that of the oracle against foreign nations. There are three major collections of these in the Old Testament: Isa. 13-23; Jer. 46-51; Ezek. 25-32. Many of these, like Isa. 47, are directed against Babylon. Most commentators trace the origins of this form back to the traditional mocking song or taunt song, somewhat akin to the curse, which was used against enemies as a powerful word whose purpose was to bring about their downfall. But in the context of Deutero-Isaiah's oracles, in which the fall of Babylon is frequently prophesied, chapter 47 is probably to be regarded, with Westermann, as prophecy addressed primarily to the Jewish exiles, intended to convince them that their deliverance from the yoke of Babylon was near. At the same time, however, it may be regarded as a 'powerful word' against Babylon itself, since we know from 55:11 that Deutero-Isaiah thought of prophecy as a word which would inevitably accomplish what Yahweh purposed.

The Composition of the Book

The final questions to be asked in this Chapter concern the process of composition of the 'book' of Deutero-Isaiah. Most modern scholars believe that these chapters attained virtually their present form before they were appended to the earlier chapters of the Book of Isaiah. The question of their relationship to the rest of the Book of Isaiah has already been touched upon and will not be pursued here except in so far as it throws light on the composition of these chapters themselves. The main questions to be asked here are who wrote down Deutero-

Isaiah's oracles and arranged them in their present form, and on what plan, if any, they are arranged. Both questions are difficult to answer.

There can be no doubt that Deutero-Isaiah's teaching, however little effect it may have had on the majority of the Jewish exiles at the time, came to be treated with great respect, at any rate in some quarters, during the immediately succeeding generations, when his prediction of the fall of Babylon to Cyrus and of the restoration of the exiled Jews to their homeland had in some measure been fulfilled. Certain passages in 'Trito-Isaiah' (Isa. 56-66) clearly indicate this: they are the work of men who regarded Deutero-Isaiah's teaching as authoritative, but who were faced with the problem of its interpretation and adaptation for their own time. Their problem was to explain why the promises remained only partially fulfilled: why, in spite of the fall of Babylon and the return of some Jews to Palestine, the expected political independence and economic prosperity had still not come about. The problems of Trito-Isaiah cannot be pursued here; but this preoccupation with the teaching of Deutero-Isaiah so soon afterwards suggests that the move towards the production of an authoritative collection of his oracles began very early. This impression is confirmed by the fact that in contrast with what occurred in the case of most of the other prophetical books, there is little trace within the 'book' itself of material added at a later time. Later comment and re-interpretation have been added for the most part not within chapters 40-55 but at the end (i.e. in chapters 56-66) of the collected oracles of the original prophet. There is, however, no evidence to show whether the prophet himself—the date of whose death is unknown—played a part in the formation of the collection.

On the question whether any consistent arrangement of the oracles can be discerned it is perhaps sufficient to say that the lack of agreement between scholars in their attempt to find one, and the failure of any of these attempts to gain widespread support, suggest a negative answer. Some indications of an editorial policy are discernible, but no more than this. It is, for example, widely agreed that the opening and concluding passages (40:1-8; 55:6-13) have been carefully chosen because they emphasize the power and authority of the word of Yahweh spoken by the prophets, so confirming the authority of the oracles placed between them. The position of 40:1-8 is also appropriate in that it is an account of the prophet's call and commissioning in the heavenly court, and contains a summary statement of his total message. It has also been observed that chapters 45-47 have the common theme of the fall of Babylon, and that the end of chapter 48 to some extent marks a thematic division of the book into two parts, although this is only partly the case.

Mowinckel (1931), admitting the impossibility of finding a logical principle of arrangement, proposed a mechanical one. He argued that the oracles have been editorially arranged on the principle of the 'catchword': passages have been juxtaposed not because of any intrinsic congruity or continuity of sense, but because of the fortuitous occurrence in both of some purely verbal link, such as the occurrence in 45:20-25 and 46:1-4 of the word 'bow down,' which however is used in two quite different senses. Even if it is possible to find some subtle theological point in this, it is a point made by an editor, since the two passages are each complete in themselves and in other respects have no thematic connection. In some cases Mowinckel's 'catchword' theory may well be correct; but his attempt to find this kind of mechanical link between every pair of passages in the book is often very forced and has failed to carry conviction.

But a logical, thematic structure is equally hard to find. Oracles which are clearly connected thematically—for example, the four so-called 'Servant Songs' (42:1-4; 49:1-6; 50:4-9; 53:1-12)—are scattered throughout the book for no clear reason, in spite of attempts to show that they are related to their contexts. It would be rash for a modern reader to assert categorically that there is no consistent, logical order in the book; but it remains the case that no attempt to discover one has so far succeeded.

Further Reading

On the form-critical study of the prophetical books in general see:

G.W. Anderson (ed.), *Tradition and Interpretation*, Oxford: Clarendon Press, 1979, chapter 6

*J.H. Hayes (ed.), *Old Testament Form Criticism*, San Antonio: Trinity University Press, 1974, chapters 1 and 4

Koch, K., *The Growth of the Biblical Tradition. The Form-Critical Method*, New York: Scribner, 1968 / London: A. & C. Black, 1969

Most of the form-critical discussions of Deutero-Isaiah as of other Old Testament books are in German. Among the most significant of these are:

H. Gressmann, 'Die literarische Analyse Deuterojesajas (Kap. 40-55),' *ZAW* 34 (1914), 254-297

L. Köhler, *Deuterojesaja stilkritisch untersucht* (BZAW 37), Giessen: Töpelmann, 1923

J. Begrich, *Studien zu Deuterojesaja*, 1938, reprinted Munich: Kaiser Verlag, 1963 (TB, 20)

H.E. von Waldow, *Anlass und Hintergrund der Verkündigung des Deuterojesaja* (dissertation, Bonn, 1953, never published yet very influential)

C. Westermann, 'Sprache und Struktur der Prophetie Deuterojesajas' in C. Westermann, *Forschungen am Alten Testament* (TB, 24), Munich: Kaiser Verlag, 1964, 72-170

More recently two studies have appeared in English which summarize the discussion of previous decades in addition to making their own contribution to it:

A. Schoors, *I Am God Your Saviour. A Form-Critical Study of the Main Genres in Is. XL-LV* (VT Suppl. 24), Leiden: Brill, 1973

R.F. Melugin, *The Formation of Isaiah 40-55* (BZAW 141), Berlin: De Gruyter, 1976

A briefer introduction to the subject is offered by:

*H.E. von Waldow, 'The Message of Deutero-Isaiah,' *Interpretation* 22 (1968), 261-287

Discussions of the wider question of the composition of the book (i.e. chapters 40-55) include:

*Muilenburg, 384-6

Melugin

Important contributions in German on this subject include:

S. Mowinckel, 'Die Komposition des deuterojesajanischen Buch,' *ZAW* 49 (1931), 87-112, 242-260

R.P. Merendino, *Der Erste und der Letzte. Eine Untersuchung von Jes 40-48* (VT Suppl. 31), Leiden: Brill, 1981

For original studies of other questions touched upon in this chapter (the origin of the oracle of salvation, the background to the trial scene, the problem of chapter 48) see the items in the Bibliography in Schoors under Begrich (1934), Boecker (1964), Harvey (1967), Westermann ('Heilswort,' 1964 and 'Jes. 48,' 1966) and Würthwein.

5

THE MESSAGE
OF DEUTERO-ISAIAH

Although Deutero-Isaiah's teaching is expressed in the form of a series of short oracles rather than of a single, systematic treatise, it possesses remarkable consistency of thought; and it is not difficult to derive from it a fully articulated theology. However, this should not be regarded in too abstract a way. His message to the exiles cannot and must not be separated from the forms of speech in which it is expressed, which themselves reflect the particular circumstances which prompted him to address them as he did. It is necessary for the student to keep these circumstances in mind if Deutero-Isaiah's theology is to be perceived for what it actually was: not an abstract exposition of doctrine, but a vital, urgent and timely message proclaimed in a time of disillusionment.

It has already been remarked that Deutero-Isaiah had two roles: that of Yahweh's messenger, conveying to the exiles what Yahweh had to say to them, and that of persuader, endeavouring to convince them of the authenticity of that message. His teaching can therefore be conveniently divided into two parts: the central message of salvation and the supporting arguments.

The Prophet's Call

But before he could even expect to gain a hearing, Deutero-Isaiah had first to present his credentials: he had to give a convincing account of how he had been called by Yahweh to be a prophet. There was nothing new about this: the books of Amos (7:14-15), Isaiah (6), Jeremiah (1:4-10) and Ezekiel (1:1-3:15) all contain accounts of those prophets' initial call to prophetic activity. Such 'call-narratives' were not mere anecdotal reminiscences but were composed in response to an urgent necessity for the prophet to authenticate his claim to be a true prophet of Yahweh, in the face of hostility or unbelief. This was equally a necessity for Deutero-Isaiah.

His account of his call stands at the beginning of the book, in 40:1-8. It differs from the call-narratives of earlier prophets in that the prophet's dialogue is apparently not with Yahweh himself but with a heavenly being or angel. In the later prophetical literature the concept of angelic intermediaries between Yahweh and his prophets, which is first discernible in Ezekiel, was to come into even greater prominence. There is however no implication that Deutero-Isaiah's authority was less directly held than, or in any way inferior to, that of earlier prophets. This is merely a shift in the way in which the mode of divine communication was understood. Deutero-Isaiah's frequent use of the messenger-formula 'Thus has Yahweh said' leaves no room for doubt that he was claiming no less an authority than that claimed by earlier prophets.

40:1-8 is set in the heavenly realms where Yahweh holds court surrounded by his heavenly servants. Deutero-Isaiah's implicit claim to have been present at this 'heavenly council' was itself a claim to prophetical status. It was at the heavenly court that Isaiah had offered himself and had been accepted as Yahweh's messenger to his people (Isa. 6), and at an earlier time still it is reported in 1 Kings 22:19-23 that the prophet Micaiah had been present in the heavenly court and had listened to Yahweh's deliberations with certain 'spirits' which attended on him. There are, moreover, two verses in the Book of Jeremiah (23:18, 22) which seem to suggest that unless a person had 'stood in the council of Yahweh' he could not be a true prophet (see Cross).

In 40:1-8 Deutero-Isaiah, like Micaiah and Isaiah before him, hears, or overhears, what is being said there. Yahweh, apparently, is not present, or at least does not speak: 'says your God' in verse 1 is part of a speech by a heavenly being, telling others 'what God is saying.' The imperatives in verses 1-3 are in the plural, addresssed not to the prophet but, it would seem, by one angel to others, conveying to them Yahweh's instructions to make preparations for his return to Jerusalem accompanied by his exiled people. But in verse 6 the imperative 'Cry!,' that is, 'Proclaim!,' is in the singular, and is answered (following a slight and generally accepted textual emendation) in the first person: 'And I said, "What shall I cry?".' This can only be the voice of Deutero-Isaiah himself: he asks what message he is to proclaim, and receives his commission. In doing so he becomes a prophet of Yahweh.

Whether Deutero-Isaiah, like some of the prophets of earlier times, has left behind him any account of later encounters with Yahweh is a question which depends on the interpretation of those passages commonly known as the 'Servant Songs.' If the person referred to, and in two cases represented as speaking, in these passages is in fact the prophet himself, they record his relations with Yahweh at various times in the course of his career. These passages will be discussed further in a later section of this Chapter.

The Central Message

Deutero-Isaiah's central message is neatly summarised in the scene in the heavenly council (40:1-8). Its essential features are:

1. The exiled people are to take heart because their sins have now been expiated and their term of punishment is over (verses 1-2).
2. Yahweh is now about to come to the aid of his people in such a decisive fashion that the whole world will be astonished at this revelation of his glory (verses 3-5).
3. The guarantee of this message of hope and restoration is the word of Yahweh spoken through the prophet, which is all-powerful, and compared with which all human activity is ludicrously impotent (verses 6-8).

This central message is spelled out in detail in other passages, especially in the salvation oracles, but also in other passages which speak of Yahweh's choice of Cyrus as his instrument, Cyrus's imminent conquest of Babylon, the release of the exiles, their triumphant return home, the rebuilding of their cities and their subsequent peaceful and prosperous life which will never again be disturbed.

The Supporting Arguments

1. *Cyrus*. The Persian king is named twice in the book, in what is probably a single oracle, 44:24-45:7. But many other passages refer to him: 41:1-5; 41:21-29; 45:9-13; 46:9-11; 48:12-16 and probably 42:5-7. These passages are of various kinds, including hymnic self-praise, disputation and trial scene. In at least one passage (45:1-7; possibly also 42:5-7) Cyrus is directly addressed and given his commission to carry out Yahweh's purpose. In all these passages Yahweh is the speaker. The meteoric military career of Cyrus, with the threat which

this posed for Babylon, was a material fact of the first importance which Deutero-Isaiah put to good use in his attempt to convince his hearers of the truth of his central message. The various types of argument which are used in this connection—arguments from prophecy, from history, from Israel's belief in Yahweh as creator of the world—will be discussed in detail later in this Chapter. But the purpose of them all was the same: to make the point that the future lay in the hands of a great and irresistible conqueror who, however, was simply an instrument of Yahweh, created by him in order to carry out his good purpose towards Israel.

Deutero-Isaiah went to great lengths to emphasize the complete dependence of Cyrus's achievements on the support given him by Yahweh. Yahweh not only calls him 'my shepherd' (44:28), a title used both in Israel and elsewhere in the ancient Near East of kings who ruled by divine appointment, but even his 'anointed one' (*māšîaḥ*, 45:1), a title which had previously been reserved exclusively for the reigning kings of the dynasty of David; he also states that he 'loves' him (48:14). The idea of Yahweh's making use of foreign kings to carry out his purpose for Israel was not in itself new; but in the past this had been in order to punish Israel for its disloyalty to Yahweh: Assyria had been 'the rod of Yahweh's anger' (Isa. 10:5-6), and Nebuchadnezzar, as Yahweh's 'servant' (Jer. 25:9; 27:6) had been sent to destroy the nation altogether. Now it was Cyrus who had been chosen as Yahweh's instrument; but Yahweh's intentions towards his people were now wholly good, and it was Babylon which was to receive the divine chastisement (48:14). The use of the title 'anointed one' is astonishing, and was no doubt intended to administer a salutary shock to those who heard it: the exiles had no anointed king of their own who could save them; but Yahweh who could do all things (45:9-13) had created one out of the unlikely material of a foreign ruler, who was already poised to deliver the blow which would open the prison gates, set the captives free (42:7; 45:2, 13; 48:14), rebuild Jerusalem and the other cities of Judah, and even lay the foundations of a restored Temple (44:26-28). The fact that Cyrus was a pagan who 'did not know' Yahweh (45:4) and might be expected to attribute his successes to his own gods was of no consequence; in any case, together with the world at large, he would eventually come to acknowledge him (45:3).

2. *The appeal to history.* Israel's pre-exilic narrative traditions, now incorporated in the biblical books from Genesis to Kings, comprised

accounts of Yahweh's great deeds in the past: his creation of the world, his guidance of the human race in its infancy, and finally his creation of Israel as his special people and his subsequent dealings with them. The Babylonian exile, because this story had now been brought to an abrupt end, was a time for reflecting on the meaning of this history, bringing together the various strands of tradition into comprehensive and theologically orientated literary works, and attempting to draw lessons, and perhaps hope, for the future from it all. Such an attempt, for the period from Moses onwards, was made at about this time by the Deuteronomist in his work which stretches from Deuteronomy to Kings; and a comparable attempt was made for the early period then or a little later by those who were responsible for the so-called 'priestly' edition of the Pentateuch. Deutero-Isaiah, who was evidently familiar with much of this material and also with some other historical allusions such as are now found in the Book of Psalms, was no exception. But his use of these traditions was somewhat different from that made by the historians: he used them as the raw material of an *appeal to history* which forms an additional argument to support his main message.

Other prophets before him had used examples from past history to illustrate their teaching, especially as dreadful warnings (e.g. Jezreel, Hos. 1:4; Sodom and Gomorrah, Isa. 1:10; the fall of Shiloh, Jer. 7:12-15; 'parables' of Israel's history in Ezekiel). Deutero-Isaiah used his examples in various ways, but above all to remind the exiles of incidents in which Yahweh had shown his power not in anger but in love towards mankind or to his people, so that his hearers could take heart and be brought to a state of mind in which they could accept that Yahweh was both willing and able to perform such deeds once more. In this he had to some extent already been anticipated by Jeremiah and Ezekiel. But in the range and number of his historical allusions—some of which are indirect, but nevertheless unmistakable—he is unequalled.

Deutero-Isaiah's use of Israel's *creation traditions* will be considered in a later section of this chapter. Apart from them, the first incident to be noted in chronological sequence is the *Flood* (54:9-10). In this passage (54:7-10) Yahweh is speaking. The question at issue is Yahweh's reliability. His aim is to persuade the exiles, who believe that, despite his covenant with them, he has forsaken them, that it is now his intention to return to them and to behave towards them with a love which will never cease: 'My steadfast love shall not depart from you, my covenant of peace shall not be removed.' In order to convince them that he will keep the oath which he has sworn to them, he uses the analogy of the oath which he swore to Noah after the Flood, that he would never again send a flood which would destroy mankind. That oath he has kept; he can therefore be relied on to keep the new one.

The next historical references are to *Abraham*. (48:18-19, a somewhat negative passage, is a reminiscence of the promises to Abraham in Gen. 22:17 and to Jacob in Gen. 32:12, but is not the work of Deutero-Isaiah.) In 51:1-3 the prophet, addressing a dispirited audience convinced that there is no hope for them in their wretched and depleted state, used the traditions of the miraculous parenthood of Abraham and Sarah and the marvellous gift to them of numerous and prosperous descendants to support the new promise that Jerusalem (Zion) will again soon be filled with a prosperous and numerous population. What Yahweh once did for their ancestors he can and will now do for them.

The other reference to Abraham (41:8) occurs in a series of epithets attached to the names Israel and Jacob at the beginning of a promise of salvation (41:8-13). This use of epithets, whether of Yahweh or of Israel, is a characteristic of Deutero-Isaiah's style. He used them to remind the exiles of facts which might dispose them to believe the promise which follows. The description of Abraham as Yahweh's 'friend' (literally, 'the one whom I loved'), which occurs again in 2 Chron. 20:7, reminds the exiles both of the intimacy and the constancy of Yahweh's love for them, which stretches back to their most remote ancestor. Deutero-Isaiah's use of the traditions about Abraham reflects a reawakened interest in the Patriarchal traditions in the period of the Exile: Abraham is never mentioned in any of the authentic oracles of the pre-exilic prophets; but Ezek. 33:24 shows that with the loss of the land of Palestine Abraham came to the fore as the ancestor whose claim to its possession remained valid for his descendants. Deutero-Isaiah's use of the Abraham traditions, however, is of a somewhat different order.

The only other reference to the patriarchal traditions is in 43:27: 'Your first father sinned.' This is almost certainly a reference to *Jacob*. Its negative view of him is also reflected in Hos. 12:3-5. The passage in which this reference occurs has already been considered (p. 35f.). In defending the Exile as a just punishment, Yahweh points out that Israel's sinful tendency manifested itself almost from the beginning. This throws an even greater emphasis on the marvel of

Yahweh's forgiveness (verse 25). 41:8 and 43:27 complement one another.

The period of Israel's history from which Deutero-Isaiah most frequently drew lessons was that of *Israel's beginnings*: the release of the nation's ancestors from slavery in Egypt, their crossing of the Red Sea, and their journey, under Yahweh's guidance, through the wilderness. These events—frequently referred to loosely as the '*Exodus events*'—offered an obvious analogy to the picture which the prophet was presenting to the exiles of what was about to happen to them. The theme had already been touched upon by Ezekiel (especially Ezek. 20:32-44), but in a very different way. Deutero-Isaiah made it his own. As with his use of other historical themes, his purpose was to convince the exiles of the truth of Yahweh's promises about the immediate future by reminding them of his great deeds in the past; but he went further than this. He taught that the 'new Exodus' (to use a convenient modern term for this theme) would be even more spectacular and lasting in its effects than the first Exodus; so much so that he could claim that Yahweh was saying (43:18-19):

> Remember not the former things,
>   nor consider the things of old.
> Behold, I am doing a new thing.

52:11-12 has the form of a command by the prophet to his fellow-exiles to begin their journey home. This is a projection into the future: he speaks as if Babylon has already fallen, or is falling, to Cyrus. They are to leave the city, preceded by the priests carrying the sacred vessels stolen by Nebuchadnezzar (verse 11), as their ancestors had been preceded by the Ark on their wilderness journeys (Num. 10:33-35). The reference to the Exodus is even clearer in verse 12. The departure from Egypt had taken place secretly, by night, and in haste. (The word 'haste' or 'hurried flight' (*hippāzōn*) used here occurs elsewhere in the Old Testament only in connection with the Exodus events—Exod. 12:11; Deut. 16:3). The departure from Babylon, on the other hand, will be more like a ceremonial procession. This verse also alludes to another Exodus motif: that of the *pillar of cloud* which went before the Israelites to guide them (Exod. 13:21-22) but moved and stood behind them to protect them against attack (Exod. 14:19-20).

Another clear allusion to the Exodus is to be found in the announcement of salvation in 43:14-21. In verses 16-17, in a series of epithets attached to the messenger-formula, Yahweh refers in plain terms, closely following the account in Exod. 14:21-29, to his *action at the Red Sea* when the Israelites were enabled to cross on dry ground while the Egyptians were drowned. This is a prelude to the admonition 'Remember not the former things': the 'new Exodus' will be far more glorious. The oracle ends with the promise proper (verses 19b-21), which speaks of a repetition of the feeding of the people of old in the wilderness during the period after the crossing of the Red Sea, rendered even more marvellous by the motif of the homage of the animal world (verse 20). Finally the crossing of the Red Sea is referred to in 51:10; but this, as has already been pointed out, is a quotation from a lamentation preceding an announcement of salvation (verse 11 is an interpolation). The latter does not specifically take up the Exodus reference from the lamentation, except perhaps in verse 15 where Yahweh speaks of stirring up the sea.

The theme of *divine guidance during the journey through the wilderness* has already been touched upon in connection with 52:11-12 and 43:19-21. It is found also in other passages. 40:3-5 and 40:9-11 speak of a triumphant march to Jerusalem led by Yahweh himself, returning to his holy city in triumph like the victor after a battle. Here the theme of guidance and protection in the wilderness has been combined with that of the divine warrior. We also find the theme of miraculous feeding during the journey again in the announcement of salvation in 41:17-20, where the miracles of the time of the old Exodus are repeated more splendidly, with the wilderness becoming a pool of water and trees springing up miraculously to provide shade. And in 42:14-17, another announcement of salvation, the whole landscape is miraculously transformed (as also in 40:3-5) to make the journey both easier and more spectacular, while darkness is turned to light (perhaps a reminiscence of the pillar of fire). There is also a reference to miraculous feeding in 48:21, which is probably, together with the previous phrase ('They thirsted not . . . '), the hymn which the returning exiles are to sing on the journey.

One further point remains to be noticed about these passages. In Exod. 14:31, after the account of the crossing of the Red Sea, it is stated that 'Israel saw the great work which Yahweh did . . . , and the people feared Yahweh, and they believed in Yahweh.' This theme of *Yahweh's glory and its effect on the beholders* is a major theme of Deutero-Isaiah's. As has been said, it was his purpose through these historical allusions to inspire confidence in the new promises which

Yahweh was now making. But this was not enough. For him the salvation of Israel was not an end in itself: the ultimate purpose was the manifestation of Yahweh's glory to the world. Deutero-Isaiah was clearly determined to turn the thoughts of the exiles away from their preoccupation with themselves to a deeper acknowledgement of the transcendent Saviour-God. It is significant that three of these passages emphasize this theme: 'And the glory of Yahweh shall be revealed' (40:5); 'that men may see and know . . . that the hand of Yahweh has done it' (41:20); ' . . . my chosen people, the people whom I formed for myself, that they might declare my praise' (43:21).

Deutero-Isaiah makes very few direct references to the *period of the monarchy*. For him as for his predecessors this was essentially a time of apostasy leading to the disruption of the kingdoms and to the Exile. Apart from a confused passage in prose (52:3-6), of which he is almost certainly not the author, which refers to the deportation of Israelites by Assyria, and an obscure reference to the fate of the Jerusalem priesthood in 43:28, the only period to which he refers directly is that of *David* (55:1-5). In this passage, in which Yahweh appeals to the exiles to detach themselves from their preoccupation with their present mode of existence and to accept the promise which is being offered to them of true satisfaction as a people restored to their own land and living in prosperity, he speaks of an 'everlasting covenant' which he will make with them, and links this with his 'steadfast, sure love for David,' the great leader of the past, whose greatness had been acknowledged by the surrounding nations. The mention of this 'golden age' of the time of David was intended to evoke the same feelings as were evoked by the references to Abraham: confidence that Yahweh who in the past had made Israel great and prosperous could and would now do so again. There is no promise here of the restoration of the Davidic dynasty: rather it is the whole people who will now be united with Yahweh, as David had been in the past, in an everlasting covenant.

As one looks back on this survey of Deutero-Isaiah's references to past history, it is clear that he had a remarkably detailed knowledge of the nation's historical traditions, and in a form which corresponds even in quite small details to the accounts which were eventually incorporated into the biblical books. Moreover, although his use of them was necessarily selective, it is equally clear that he was able to see the history of Israel as a continuous whole. He was very aware that, despite the terrible interval of the Exile, there was a continuity in Yahweh's dealings with his people: it was not Yahweh who had ceased to love and care for his people, but Israel which had ceased to love Yahweh. Yahweh is consistently pictured as always ready to demonstrate his love for Israel, and now even more abundantly than before.

3. *The interpretation of Israel's sufferings.* It was not enough for Deutero-Isaiah to draw these lessons from the past. It was above all the sufferings and disappointments of the present which made the exiles reluctant to believe in the readiness of Yahweh to help them. Deutero-Isaiah had to interpret these sufferings: he had to account for them, and also to convince his audience that they were now coming to an end.

Firstly, he emphasized that it was Yahweh who had inflicted them: it was not the Babylonian kings, who were only Yahweh's instruments, and certainly not their seemingly all-powerful gods. The point was not a new one: it had been made, *mutatis mutandis*, by both the eighth and the seventh-century prophets both in warnings and in comments on past disasters. Deutero-Isaiah made it in a characteristic way in 42:18-25, sometimes classified as a trial scene against Israel. In verses 18-20 he depicts a nation so stupid that they had been unable to see that what was happening to them was the result of their sin. A similar point is made in 43:22-24 (on this passage see above, pp. 35f.).

But to tell the exiles that they deserved what they had got was to risk leaving them in despair, and also to leave them still with the feeling that Yahweh was unfair to them, since the generation whose behaviour had led to the Exile was now dead, and the new generation felt (as we learn from other exilic writings such as Jer. 31:29; Ezek. 18:2-4; Lam. 5:7) that they were being punished for their parents' sins. Deutero-Isaiah's answer was to assure them that it was precisely the new generation which was to be treated differently from that of their parents. The sufferings of the Exile had never been intended by Yahweh to last for ever. He had always intended that they should have a limit; and that limit had now been reached. The 'sentence of imprisonment' had been served: and the exiles were therefore about to become free men again (40:1-2). This is also the point of the passage about the supposed 'divorce' between Yahweh and his people (50:1, also part of a supposed 'trial scene'). Hosea (2:2), Jeremiah (3:8) and Ezekiel (16) had all used the metaphor of divorce to stress that Yahweh had rejected his people and broken the relationship between him and them. They had, it is true, envisaged the possibility of a reconciliation. Deutero-Isaiah, however, seems in 50:1 to have denied that there had ever been a real divorce: since there is no 'divorce certificate' (see Deut. 24:1-4; Jer. 3:8), there had only been a temporary separation.

Another problem which had much exercised earlier prophets, especially Ezekiel, was the question of repentance. The pre-exilic prophets had made repentance a condition of reconciliation with Yahweh. But there was not really any sign that the people had repented. How, then, could it be asserted that Yahweh had forgiven them? In answer to this problem Deutero-Isaiah stressed the *grace* of Yahweh which does not wait for repentance. Here, as so often, he comes closer to the New Testament than any other Old Testament teacher. This is most clearly seen in 43:22-28, which has been already discussed, where in verse 25 a declaration of free pardon is given in an oracle which begins as an oracle of judgement. Deutero-Isaiah's theology is a theology of grace which outweighs all other considerations.

To sum up: Deutero-Isaiah dealt with the problem of Israel's sufferings in exile by asserting that these were not due to external powers which Yahweh was unable to control, but to Yahweh himself; by interpreting them as a divine punishment justly inflicted; and by claiming that they were intended to have a limit, which had now been reached. He also overcame the argument that there can be no reconciliation with God without national repentance by preaching a doctrine of the unconditional grace of a God who continues to love his people and will always do so.

4. *Yahweh as creator and only God.* In spite of their traditional belief, expressed in psalms and creation-narratives, that Yahweh was the creator of the world, the Jewish exiles in Babylon, surrounded by the grandiose worship of the Babylonian gods, to whom of course the Babylonians attributed their conquests, were easily tempted to wonder whether their own beliefs were mistaken: whether their humiliation was due to Yahweh's having been defeated by gods more powerful than himself. These doubts would have been nourished by the celebration of the annual New Year Festival at Babylon, a festival which commemorated the creation of the world by Marduk, his installation as king of the gods, and the supremacy of his city, Babylon. Although the actual rites of this festival were celebrated in private, there were public processions along the great sacral way, and the festival was the occasion of public rejoicing. Moreover it is probable that the Babylonian

creation myths such as the 'Creation Epic' (*Enuma Elish*), which describes Marduk's exploits (Pritchard, 60-72; *Thomas, 3-16), were familiar to the ordinary citizens through public recitation. Festivals and myths alike must have seemed to the Jewish exiles to correspond to the political reality of Babylon's supremacy.

How could Deutero-Isaiah combat the effects of this pro-Marduk propaganda? It can of course never be proved beyond doubt that one religion is true and another false. All that the prophet could do was to set the mythological tradition of Babylon against the more sober theological tradition of Israel, and to attempt to show in point after point that the latter was more credible than the former. In addition to rational argument, he also used his poetical skill to evoke the mood of joyful confidence in Yahweh's incomparable power and majesty which had been the keynote of the Judaean festival cult in the days when Yahweh's kingship had been celebrated in Jerusalem. It was in the performance of this task that Deutero-Isaiah produced some of his finest poems.

In 40:12-31 he used the disputation form as the vehicle for his arguments. In the first of these disputations (verses 12-17) he restated the Israelite creation tradition in a series of rhetorical questions in order to make the point that if it is indeed Yahweh who created the world of nature with such skill (verses 12-14) he must also possess absolute control over his human creatures, and so over the historical process (verses 15-17). The implication, clear though not directly stated, is that Babylon, far from being the undisputed mistress of the world, is in fact powerless and insignificant, no obstacle to Yahweh's plans. This theological point, arguing from belief in Yahweh as creator to belief in his control of history, may seem obvious now. But it was not always obvious; and although the link between the two themes had not gone entirely unperceived before the time of Deutero-Isaiah, it had never before been so clearly expressed.

But this disputation also puts forward an argument to show that the Israelite creation tradition itself is superior to that of Babylon. In verses 13-14 the question is asked, rhetorically, whether Yahweh had needed help to carry out his work of creation. This is an indirect allusion to the Babylonian polytheistic tradition such as is found in *Enuma Elish*, where Marduk, himself appointed as king by a 'committee' of gods, nevertheless received help in his creative work from the wise Ea, his father, who is in fact alone credited in one passage with the creation of mankind. None of the Babylonian gods therefore could be 'God' in an absolute sense as was Yahweh, to whom therefore Deutero-Isaiah can simply refer absolutely as 'God' (e.g. in verse 18). The implication is clear: the Israelite tradition of a sole creator is the one which has the ring of truth.

40:18-26 (omitting verses 19-20 which have been interpolated) also begins with a question (verse 18) which raises even more specifically the issue of Yahweh's incomparability. The background, once more, is Babylon's polytheism, whose gods, in spite of their different characteristics, were all comparable to one another in that they all belonged to the category 'god.' It would have been easy for the Jewish exiles similarly to come to regard Yahweh as a 'god' like any other: to reduce him to the level of one 'god' among many.

In verse 21 comes a series of further questions, which are in fact reproaches: Deutero-Isaiah asks his audience how they can possibly be in any doubt about Yahweh's incomparability. Surely they know their own tradition! In verse 22 he reminds them of that tradition, using the participial style and vocabulary of the creation hymn (cf. Pss. 136 and 104, especially 104:2b, which is almost identical with part of this verse). Then, as in verses 12-17, he turns from the theme of the creation of the world to that of Yahweh's power over the rulers and nations of the world: since it is Yahweh who created the world, the political power of Babylon (and other nations) must also be entirely subject to him and can be brought to an end whenever he wishes.

The concluding verse (26) about Yahweh and the heavenly bodies may at first seem to be an anticlimax; but in fact it is equally polemical. In *Enuma Elish* (Tablet V) the heavenly bodies are not Marduk's creatures: they are the great gods themselves. Marduk established them in the heavens with their prescribed movements, but they were still gods. Marduk was neither an absolute monarch nor a sole god. Against this polytheistic belief Deutero-Isaiah set the monotheistic Israelite tradition. The heavenly bodies are simply Yahweh's creatures. He uses the special word *bārā'*, 'create,' here, a word which is used only of divine creation, and so makes an absolute distinction between creator and creatures. Having created the heavenly bodies Yahweh put them, as it were, 'on parade,' bringing them out to shine 'by number.' 'Not one is missing.' Yahweh, then, really is incomparable: for him there are no divine rivals. It is interesting to note that the 'priestly' writer, Deutero-Isaiah's contemporary or near-contemporary, made exactly the same point in Gen. 1:14-18, and that he too used the verb *bārā'* for exactly the same purpose.

In the final disputation in this series (verses 27-31) Deutero-Isaiah appeals to the traditional understanding of Yahweh as creator in order to answer a specific complaint, similar in form to many complaints in the lamentations in the Book of Psalms: that Yahweh either does not know about the exiles' situation, or is ignoring it. The first of these charges he dismisses as ludicrous. As for the second, for the creature to demand immediate action from the creator in this way is a presumptuous denial of his essential unknowability and betrays a lack of trust. Those who 'wait for him' will find that he will not fail them.

The polemic against Babylonian polytheism is taken up again in 43:10-13, part of a trial scene (verses 8-13) in which Yahweh is the speaker. Yahweh's claim, which follows Israel's traditional belief, is that 'Before me no god was formed, nor shall there be any after me' (verse 10). This is a clear allusion to Babylonian mythology, according to which Marduk belonged not to the first but to the fourth generation of gods (*Enuma Elish*, Tablet I), his father, Ea, and his mother Damkina being mentioned by name. Marduk himself had children: so there were gods before Marduk was born, and gods after him. Deutero-Isaiah is, by implication, asking his audience which they would rather believe: the fairy-tale mythology of Babylon, or their own tradition of Yahweh who had existed since eternity and would always exist: the only god, without birth and without sexuality. The phrase 'I am He' (verse 13 and repeated frequently in other passages) means in effect 'I am the Only One.' Deutero-Isaiah pursues the argument: the sole creator must also be the sole saviour: there is no other god to hinder him from saving his people. A similar point is made in 44:6-8; 44:24; 45:5; 46:9; 51:6.

The Israelite belief in Yahweh as creator is also made the basis of some of Deutero-Isaiah's other leading arguments. As has already been pointed out, he used it in 45:9-13 (a disputation in which Yahweh is the speaker) to defend Yahweh's right as creator to do whatever he wishes with his creatures, as does a potter with his pots or a father with his children. The point here, as the final verse makes clear, is Yahweh's choice of the foreign king Cyrus as his instrument in the salvation and restoration of Israel, a choice which will certainly have needed some defence. Again in 54:16-17, in a passage (verses 11-17) promising the rebuilding of Jerusalem and the blessedness of the life of the future restored community, he assures the sceptical exiles that they will never again have to fear enemy attacks because Yahweh is the creator both of every imaginable enemy and also of all swordsmiths whose products might be used against Israel: once again, creatorship is held to imply total control over the actions of the creature.

Finally Deutero-Isaiah used the doctrine of creation to support his teaching about the efficacy of the prophetic word. In 45:18-19 he began from the purposefulness of Yahweh's act of creation of the world: he created it not to be a chaos but to be inhabited—a very different view of mankind from that of the Babylonians, for whom man's sole duty was to act as slave to the gods. Deutero-Isaiah argued that the same purposefulness is to be seen in the word which Yahweh speaks through the prophets. The references to 'speaking in secret' and in 'a land of darkness' are probably allusions to Babylonian divination, in contrast to which Yahweh has always spoken out clearly and openly. The conclusion is that the exiles can rely on what he is saying through his prophet now. The use of the argument from creation in 55:8-11, where an analogy is drawn between the fertilising activity of the rain sent from heaven and Yahweh's prophetic word, has already been referred to (p. 38).

Deutero-Isaiah, then, used the Israelite creation traditions in a number of different ways in his attempt to convince the exiles of the truth of his basic message of imminent salvation: he used them to expose the absurdity of Babylonian polytheism, to show that it was Yahweh who possesses sole control over world history, and to stimulate trust in Yahweh and in the word of promise which he was speaking through his prophet.

5. *The argument from prophecy*. As a further way of showing that it was Yahweh and Yahweh alone who possessed control over history and therefore could claim to be the only true God, Deutero-Isaiah devised a test: if it could be shown that a god knew in advance that certain events would take place, then it could reasonably be claimed that it was he who had caused them to happen. That proof Deutero-Isaiah found in the phenomenon of prophecy, a phenomenon which was to all intents and purposes unique to Israel. The Babylonians, of course, claimed control over history for their own gods: Nebuchadnezzar, for example, claimed on his memorial stelae that it was Marduk who had given him his victories. But what proof could they offer?

Deutero-Isaiah's own argument, based on Yahweh's prediction of events through his prophets, is set out in the trial scenes to which reference has already been made. 41:21-29 will serve as an example. First, the scene is set (verse 21). This is, as has already been said, a kind of 'fact finding tribunal' at which the question 'Who is the true God?' is to be settled. Yahweh is the convener, and he begins by addressing the heathen gods. They are invited to show how in the past they had predicted the future; or, if they cannot do that, at least to make an attempt to predict the future now. This will show them to be gods (verse 23). But they are silent; and it must therefore be concluded that they are 'nothing.' This imaginary scene provides a suitable setting for Yahweh to state his own case (from verse 25). He refers to the career of Cyrus, asks who predicted it (verse 26), and himself gives the answer: no-one but himself. This evidently refers to some earlier prophecies; and this reference creates a problem, since it is not possible to point with certainty to such prophecies of the career of Cyrus within the extant prophetical books of the Old Testament. Nevertheless we can take it for granted that Deutero-Isaiah's listeners must have been familiar with such prophecies, since otherwise the passage makes no sense. Such prophecies would, in any case, be entirely consistent with the predictive activity by prophets of future events of which there are many other examples in the Old Testament. The trial scene concludes (verses 28-29) with a reiteration of the conclusion that the heathen gods are 'nothing.'

Similar arguments are to be found in other trial scenes in the book, some of which contain additional features: for example, in 43:8-13 the tribunal summons witnesses to support the arguments, the worshippers of the heathen gods on one side and Yahweh's witnesses, that is, Israel, on the other.

6. *The argument from idol worship.* Attacking Babylonian religion from another angle, Deutero-Isaiah, following the precedent of earlier prophets, seized upon an essential difference between Babylonian and Israelite worship: the absence, in the latter, of a divine image. Although the Old Testament frequently speaks of tendencies towards idolatry and even, at certain periods, of its widespread practice in Israel, these were departures from the norm, the prohibition of divine images set out in the Decalogue (Exod. 20:4-6; Deut. 5:8-10). Imageless worship was thus a fundamental characteristic of Israelite religious practice, and Deutero-Isaiah realized both its theological significance and its polemical value. Most if not all the other religions of the ancient Near East involved the making and worship of the statues of their gods, and the Babylonians in particular attached great importance to this.

It would be inappropriate to ask here whether the Babylonians and other ancient peoples identified the statues of their gods totally with the gods themselves: religious beliefs are usually complex and intuitive, and cannot easily be reduced to simple logical formulae. But Deutero-Isaiah did ask that question, and he answered it, rightly or wrongly, in the affirmative. The Babylonians did, after all, make images of their gods and offer worship to them. To an Israelite for whom the divinity and sovereignty of the one true God was symbolized precisely by his invisibility and intangibility, such behaviour was not only blasphemous but also ludicrous.

Deutero-Isaiah inherited a tradition in which worshippers of idols were mocked for 'worshipping the works of their own hands' (Isa. 2:8; compare Hos. 13:2; Hab. 2:18-19; Ps. 97:7 and—though probably from a later period—Ps. 115:4-8; 135:15-18). He carried the mockery further by describing in some detail the effort put into the manufacture of idols (40:19-20; 41:6-7). These descriptions bear some similarity to a Babylonian text (Pritchard, 331-2) which contains instructions to craftsmen pursuing this craft; and it has even been suggested that the prophet may himself have witnessed such men at work in some small idol-factory. The tone is contemptuous. He lays great stress on two facts: that the idol owes its existence to nothing more supernatural than the market demand, and that it is rigid and unable to move. (44:9-20 is an even more explicit satire on this subject, though this passage, which is in prose, is probably not the work of Deutero-Isaiah himself.)

Finally there is a rather different, and theologically more important, passage on this subject in 46:1-4. This is one of the most effective of Deutero-Isaiah's poems. It consists of two contrasting sections. Verses 1-2 are concerned with the two principal Babylonian gods, Bel (Marduk) and Nebo (Nabu), verses 3-4 with Yahweh. The contrast between the two sections is brought out by the use of the verbs 'carry' and 'bear.' The scene depicted in the first part belongs to the immediate future which has been promised: Babylon is falling; and the worshippers of its gods are loading them—that is, their statues—on beasts of burden in an attempt to escape from the city with them. The point is cleverly made that these gods, who have always been worshipped and revered as great gods who by their immense power will always act to protect the city, are in fact so useless that they have now become a burden to their own worshippers: they have to be carried—and very heavy they are! The Hebrew here contrives to convey the impression of men sweating and grunting as they try to move these dead weights.

In contrast with this scene, in the second section (verses 3-4) Yahweh speaks to his people and reminds them that, far from being a burden to them, *he* has always carried *them*—that is, he has protected and helped them: they have been his burden. The passage concludes with a promise that he will continue to 'carry' them: 'even to your old age.' Here as elsewhere in the book the themes of Yahweh's power to save and his willingness to do so are linked together against the background of the uselessness of the outwardly splendid and victorious gods of Babylon.

7. *The redeeming God.* The most profound of all the arguments which Deutero-Isaiah used to persuade his fellow-exiles to believe his message was based on the nature of Yahweh himself. Over and over again, in direct address to the exiles, Yahweh reveals his inner motives. It is not merely that he is able to help his people, or that he is willing to do so, or that he can point to his record of earlier kindness towards them. His true motive springs from something mysterious and inexplicable: his inexhaustible love for them. In the desperate situation in which the exiles find themselves at present, this love must and will find its expression in the nation's redemption and restoration. For Deutero-Isaiah, then, Yahweh is above all a redeeming God: a God who without waiting for national repentance will take the initiative and, simply out of love for his people, act to save them.

This note of *unconditional* love for a sinful and still unrepentant people is hardly to be found in the pre-exilic prophets, except perhaps in Hosea, who pictures Yahweh as offering a new betrothal to his faithless wife Israel (Hos. 2:14-17). Otherwise, in those passages generally regarded as authentic, these prophets represented Yahweh as offering a hope of rescue or restoration only on condition of a whole-hearted return to him in submission to his will. In the exilic period, with Jeremiah (31:31-34) and Ezekiel (36:25-27; 37:1-14), the note of divine grace was sounded more clearly. In these passages, with their images of a new heart, a new spirit and a new covenant, there is a recognition that Israel is incapable of taking any steps to save itself, and that therefore redemption can only take the form of something quite new: a new beginning, the creation of a new Israel, whose nature will be innately disposed towards obedience to its creator. This teaching clearly foreshadows that of Deutero-Isaiah.

Nevertheless, in Ezekiel at least, this new creation is not attributed to feelings of tenderness and love on the part of Yahweh. Rather Ezekiel represents him as acting according to his own interests: 'It is not for your sake, O house of Israel, that I am about to act, but for the sake of my holy name, which you have profaned' (Ezek. 36:22). There is an echo of this in Isa. 48:9, 11; but this passage is almost certainly an interpolation and not the work of Deutero-Isaiah. It is not representative of his teaching. For him all the emphasis is on Yahweh's love for his people which moves him to come to their aid. It is true that the ultimate goal of his redemptive activity lies beyond the confines of Israel: it is his intention that 'they [i.e. mankind] may see and know . . . that it is the hand of Yahweh who has done this' (41:20). Nevertheless Deutero-Isaiah again and again, in passages too numerous to list here, stresses Yahweh's love and forgiveness towards his people.

Like Jeremiah and Ezekiel, Deutero-Isaiah apparently saw no real sign of repentance on the part of the exiles. Passages like 42:24-25 should perhaps be understood as referring principally to past generations rather than to the present one; but throughout the oracles, especially in the references to their lamentations and in the disputations, the exiles are explicitly or implicitly reproached for their lack of faith; and in some passages (e.g. 55:6-7) they are addressed as not yet having sincerely submitted themselves to Yahweh. But, again like Jeremiah and Ezekiel, Deutero-Isaiah did not regard repentance as a precondition for Yahweh's forgiveness; rather it would be the consequence of forgiveness: 'Return to me, for I have redeemed you' (44:22).

The verb *gā'al*, rendered in the above passage by 'redeemed,' is used several times by Deutero-Isaiah to refer to Yahweh's action in rescuing his people. Particularly striking is his frequent use (41:14; 43:14; 44:6, 24; 47:4; 48:17; 49:7, 26; 54:5, 8) of the related noun (strictly a participle) *gō'ēl*, 'redeemer,' as a kind of title of Yahweh, indicating that his redemptive role is not an exceptional or a secondary one, but one which belongs to the essence of his relationship with Israel: Yahweh is 'the Redeemer of Israel.' In Israelite family law (see especially Lev. 25:25-55) the *gō'ēl* was the kinsman who rescued his relatives from economic difficulties which might otherwise lead to enslavement for debt. The application of this term to the action of Yahweh in coming to the rescue of his people is virtually peculiar to Deutero-Isaiah; and the degree of condescension shown by Yahweh in assuming this role is further emphasized by the fact that in these passages Yahweh is also described by the exalted title of 'the Holy One of Israel': 'your Redeemer is the Holy One of Israel' (41:14).

Elsewhere in the oracles other comparable terms are used to express this redemptive role: Yahweh is Israel's helper or 'saviour' (*mōšiaʿ*); he is like a shepherd to them, etc. The prophet also speaks explicitly of his 'great compassion' and his 'everlasting love' (54:7-8). Like Hosea and Jeremiah he speaks of Israel as the estranged wife whom Yahweh will restore to himself (e.g. 54:5-6). The keynote which is struck in the very first oracle (40:1-2) with its message of comfort and assurance of forgiveness dominates the entire book right to the end.

It has already been pointed out that Deutero-Isaiah used the Israelite belief in Yahweh as the Creator of the world as a basis for his demonstration that he possesses the power to redeem his people, and also that he saw the coming act of redemption as the creation of a new Israel. So it may be said that a further aspect of his understanding of Yahweh as Redeemer is that, for him, Yahweh's redemptive and creative actions are parts of a single whole. Yahweh was Creator of the world, creator of Israel, and also creator of the 'new things' which were now being announced. In a number of passages (42:9; 43:18-19; 48:3, 6) these 'new things' are contrasted with the 'former things' which Yahweh had done in the past. The latter, though in themselves wonderful, now merely serve as foils for the even greater 'new things' about to be done. The word 'new' is a key word in Deutero-Isaiah's doctrine of redemption, and even when the word itself is not used the idea is often present. The modern phrases 'new Exodus,' 'new creation,' 'new Israel' are not Deutero-Isaiah's own; but their use is justified in that they express succinctly what Deutero-Isaiah was saying.

The ultimate aim of Yahweh's redemptive activity, however, is the manifestation of his glory (40:3-5; 41:17-20; 43:5-7). In 42:7-9 Yahweh states specifically that he is jealous for his reputation and that he will not allow other gods to take his glory from him. God is all; man exists to glorify him. Man's enjoyment of his favour is not an end in itself.

A Mission to the Gentiles?

What place, if any, were the other nations of the world to be given in this scheme of redemption? Many scholars, following an interpretative tradition of great antiquity, have held that Deutero-Isaiah believed Israel to have been entrusted by Yahweh with a 'mission to the Gentiles,' to convert them to the Jewish faith. H.H. Rowley, for example, wrote of his 'conception of Israel as the Servant, charged with a mission to bring all men to the true religion' (Rowley, 1952, 53).

Others (e.g. de Boer, Orlinsky, Snaith) have equally denied this. The view of Israel as a missionary nation is to a large extent dependent on a particular interpretation of the figure of Yahweh's 'Servant' in Deutero-Isaiah, a matter which will be considered below. But his oracles contain numerous references to the nations which are unconnected with the role of the Servant, and these must be given due weight in the discussion.

The majority of the references in the book to the nations are either contemptuous or hostile. Some refer to Cyrus's conquests, carried out through Yahweh's enabling power (41:2-3, 25; 45:1-3; 48:14), or to the imminent fall of Babylon (43:14; 46:1-2). Chapter 47, addressed to Babylon, shows no pity for its inhabitants. Other oracles are expressed in more general terms. A number of passages speak of the discomfiture of any enemy, present or future, who may attack Israel (41:11-13; 49:26; 51:7-8, 23; 54:15). 49:7 and 49:22-23 go further: here it is predicted that foreign kings and rulers, conquered by Israel, will present themselves as suppliants in chains, prostrating themselves to Israel and becoming its slaves. There is a similar picture in 45:14. In 43:3-4, in highly imaginative imagery, Yahweh goes as far as to say that Israel is so precious to him that the other nations are expendable, fit only to be used as counters to be exchanged in order to save Israel, which is now held to ransom. Such passages seem to hark back to the imperialist days of David and Solomon rather than to look forward to an era in which the other nations will share Yahweh's protection equally with Israel. Indeed, several oracles culminate in statements difficult to reconcile with the latter idea, e.g. 'I will put salvation in Zion, for Israel my glory' (46:13); 'In Yahweh all the offspring of Israel shall triumph and glory' (45:25).

Some passages, however, have frequently been interpreted in an universalistic sense. One of these is 45:14, mentioned above. Here a number of foreign nations acknowledge the God of Israel as the only God. But as this confession is made by prisoners of war kneeling in chains before their Israelite conqueror, the situation can hardly be seen as an example of Israel's mission to the nations. This is rather an example of Israelite imperialism, spiritual as well as military. In contrast, 44:5 does refer to foreigners who, seeing Israel's prosperity, will seek membership of the chosen people. However, it is clear that they come as individuals. This is an example, not of the mass conversion of the nations, but of what was later to be called the admission of proselytes to the fellowship of Israel. On the other hand 45:22, though frequently so interpreted (e.g. by Westermann, 1969) is not in any way concerned with religious conversion, national or individual. This trial scene (45:20-25) emphasizes the triumph of Yahweh together with that of Yahweh's chosen people Israel. That this triumph will be acknowledged by the whole universe is one of Deutero-Isaiah's recurring themes (compare, for example, 40:5); but this is not the 'universal salvation' envisaged by some interpreters. There is no good reason to take the phrase 'all the ends of the earth' as referring to the nations: if it refers specifically to human beings rather than to the whole created universe, the most probable reference is to the Jews now scattered among the nations (compare its use in 43:6-7). The situation envisaged is the same as in 55:5. (On this question see the discussions cited in my commentary, 111-112.)

It may be thought that the passages which refer to Cyrus and his special dependence on Yahweh (see above, pp. 45ff.), especially the statement in 45:3 that Cyrus, though now unaware of this dependence (verse 4), will eventually come to recognize it, have a universalistic flavour. But it is significant that Deutero-Isaiah makes nothing more of this theme. He does not say that Cyrus—or his people the Persians, who are never mentioned—will abandon his own religion in favour of the worship of Yahweh. Cyrus's eventual acknowledgement of Yahweh's universal power is mentioned only as an example of the submission to Yahweh's dominion of the whole of creation. Deutero-Isaiah's interest in Cyrus is confined to his role as the instrument of the exiles' liberation and restoration.

The texts which more than any others have given rise to the view that Deutero-Isaiah thought of Israel as a missionary to the nations still remain to be considered. Two of them (42:1-4 and 49:1-6) belong to the group of passages known as the 'Servant Songs.' A third, 42:5-9, is generally considered to be an independent oracle, although some scholars have held it to be a continuation of 42:1-4. The identity of the 'Servant' will be discussed below. However, his supposed missionary role, whether he stands for Israel or is a historical individual, may legitimately be examined independently of this question. The issue turns on the interpretation of particular words and phrases in the following sentences:

> He shall bring forth 'judgement' (*mišpāṭ*) to the nations
> (42:1)
> Until he has set 'judgement' (*mišpāṭ*) in the earth (42:4)

The coastlands shall wait for his 'law' (*tōrāh*) (42:4)
I have made you a 'covenant of (the) people' (*bᵉrît ʿām*), a light of
   nations (42:6)
I will make you a light of nations, so that my 'salvation' (*yᵉšūʿāh*)
   may reach to the end of the earth (49:6)

It is difficult for a modern reader to dissociate these phrases from
their traditional Christian interpretation; yet in fact none of the
words rendered by judgement, law, light, salvation in the above
quotations necessarily suggests, in the original Hebrew, a mission to
convert the nations. Judgement and law most naturally refer to
Yahweh's universal sovereignty; 'salvation' in Deutero-Isaiah frequently means 'victory'—that is, the victory which saves Israel from
a state of slavery. 'Covenant of the people' would require a somewhat
forced translation of a singular noun (*ʿam*, 'people') to make it refer
to a plurality of nations; and 'a light of the nations' is obscure and not
an obvious term for religious conversion.

The above examination of the relevant texts reveals very little
evidence in favour of the view that Deutero-Isaiah saw Israel as
commissioned by Yahweh to be a missionary people. Even in 44:5, in
which he prophesies that foreigners will plead to be permitted, as
individuals, to enter into the full membership of the chosen people,
he is clearly concerned to depict Israel as the envy of the world rather
than to see this development as in itself the fulfilment of Yahweh's
universal purpose.

The Servant of Yahweh

It is one of the special features of the oracles of Deutero-Isaiah that
Israel as a nation is frequently referred to as Yahweh's 'servant' or
'slave' (*ʿebed*). This epithet of Israel, though virtually peculiar to
Deutero-Isaiah, does not call for special remark. Both in the Old
Testament and in the literature of the ancient Near East generally,
those who 'served,' that is, acknowledged and worshipped, a particular
deity were commonly referred to as that deity's 'servants.' In the Old
Testament the term is especially used to designate individual persons
whose attachment to Yahweh was especially noteworthy, such as
Abraham, Moses or David. It is also used of prophets (1 Kings 18:36;
Amos 3:7; Jer. 7:25). Deutero-Isaiah's designation of the nation Israel
as Yahweh's servant is an example of his general tendency to personify
the nation as a single individual. He used this term especially in the
salvation oracles (e.g. 41:8-10) to remind the exiles of their special

relationship with Yahweh and so to give them confidence in his good will towards them.

The Servant Songs

There are, however, a number of other passages which speak of a Servant of Yahweh but do not unmistakably identify him with Israel. Some of these refer to him in vivid personal terms and attribute to him an active role which is in marked contrast with that assigned to the Servant-Israel in the first group of passages, which is simply to wait expectantly for Yahweh to come and save him. This raises a question of fundamental importance for the interpretation of the oracles as a whole: is the Servant always Israel despite this duality of role, or was Deutero-Isaiah speaking in this second group of oracles about a different figure—perhaps about some individual person who, like a Moses or a David or one of the prophets, merited this exceptional title? Such a person would clearly be a key figure in Deutero-Isaiah's conception of Israel's redemption.

The interpretation of the Servant in some passages as an individual is at least as old as the question put by the Ethiopian eunuch about the interpretation of Isa. 53:7-8 in Acts 8:34. But in 1892 Bernhard Duhm put the matter in a new and precise way. He singled out four passages (42:1-4; 49:1-6; 50:4-9; 52:13-53:12) in which a single *individual* 'Servant of Yahweh' is to be seen, sharply distinguishing these from the remainder of the book, in which the Servant is Israel. These four passages he called 'Servant Songs' (*Ebed-Lieder*). Although his view about the identity of this individual Servant has not met with general acceptance, his theory that these four passages constitute a distinct group within the book has been so influential that all subsequent discussion of the Servant of Yahweh in Deutero-Isaiah has been obliged to take it into account. Some attempts have been made since to add further passages to the list or to include additional verses (e.g. extending the first 'Song' to 42:7), but these have not been generally accepted. The discussion which follows will therefore be restricted to Duhm's original four. (Further study of this question should begin with North, 1948.)

The following summary of the contents of the 'Servant Songs' is intended to illustrate Duhm's theory and also to provide a basis for the discussion of the identity of their central figure.

1. 42:1-4

Yahweh here makes a declaration (to an unnamed audience) in support of his Servant: he has chosen him himself and is confident that, in the strength of his own Spirit, which he has bestowed on him, he will be able to carry out the task which he has assigned to him. This is to give to the nations of the world *mišpāṭ*, probably 'judgement' rather than 'justice' (see pp. 64f. above), and 'his *tōrāh*,' that is, his (the Servant's) authoritative instruction or law (verses 1b, 4). He will work quietly and gently (verses 2-3), but nothing will prevent his success (verse 4a). Nothing is said in this passage about a task to be performed for Israel, unless the phrases 'bruised reed' and 'dimly burning wick' (verse 3) refer to the weak state of the exiles' faith in Yahweh.

2. 49:1-6

Now the Servant himself speaks, addressing the inhabitants of the world. He refers first to his earlier experiences, beginning with his summons by Yahweh to be his Servant, which took place even before he was born (verses 1b, 3). In verse 2 he refers to the work which he was empowered to do: to speak words of power, comparable to using a sharp sword; he describes himself similarly as a sharp arrow. The purpose of this task was that Yahweh's glory should be made known. He then (verse 4a) reports that his earlier work had ended in apparent failure, though he had never doubted that Yahweh was on his side (verse 4b). Finally he announces that Yahweh has now spoken to him again, confirming his original task (verses 5a, 6a) but also giving him an additional and greater one (verse 6b). The original task had been given him solely for the benefit of Israel—for the revival of the stricken nation; the new one (virtually the same as is described in 42:1-4) was to impose the recognition of Yahweh's sovereignty on the whole world. It seems clear that these two passages belong to different stages in the career of the same person.

One important point remains to be noticed in 49:1-6: in verse 3 the Servant is specifically identified with Israel. But the matter is not as simple as it might seem, for a not inconsiderable number of scholars believe that the word 'Israel' here is a later addition to the original text. The reasons for this opinion will be discussed below (pp. 70f.)

3. 50:4-9

In this passage the Servant (though here not specifically so designated) again speaks of his task and of his trust in Yahweh's support. As in the other two passages his task is to speak words given him by Yahweh (verses 4, 5), but now these are words of consolation addressed to 'the weary' (who are not further defined). He again reports apparent failure, but this time in specific terms: his message has been received with open hostility and physical assault (verses 6-8).

4. 52:13—53:12

There are many unsolved problems regarding the interpretation of several parts of this passage. First in 52:13-15 (which some interpreters, unlike Duhm, regard as a separate oracle) Yahweh himself speaks (part of verse 14, from 'his appearance' to 'sons of men,' has been misplaced from the end of 53:2). He promises the Servant a future status so exalted that even kings will be astonished at him. Then in 53:1 a group of people ('we') begin to speak about the Servant. They first express their astonishment at some news which has just reached them: the Servant, whom they had always believed to be a wretch afflicted by God with a particularly horrible punishment, has now been rescued from danger by Yahweh himself ('the arm of Yahweh') (53:1-2; 52:14b; 53:3). In the light of this news they confess their earlier erroneous assessment of him (verses 4-6): they now realize that there has been a divine purpose in his suffering, and that from this they have in some way benefited. The situation is the reverse of what they had supposed: they are the guilty ones, while he is innocent. They then refer (verses 7-9) to his suffering, and also (according to many interpreters) to his consequent death. The Hebrew text of verse 10 as far as 'an offering for sin' is unfortunately very muddled and impossible to translate with any certainty; but verses 10b-12 return to the subject of the Servant's future triumph in terms reminiscent of 52:13-15. Yahweh is once more speaking; and he promises the Servant the reward of a happy life for his willingness to bear, and to bear to the end, an undeserved penalty for sins committed by others.

Who is the Servant?

However one evaluates the traditional Christian view that the portrait of the Servant is in some way the portrait of Jesus of Nazareth who lived many centuries later than the author of the Songs, it is reasonable to suppose that Deutero-Isaiah's primary intention was to portray a figure which had some immediate significance for his own contemporaries.

The problem of identification faced by subsequent generations of readers is due mainly to the loss of the key to the language in which the Servant Songs are couched. Like many other ancient poetical texts which presumably presented no difficulties to their original readers, the Songs have become obscure to those who do not share their background. The author described the Servant in such a bewildering assortment of images that many different interpretations can each find its own textual support. Some scholars (e.g. Westermann, Clines) consider that the imprecision of the outlines of the figure is deliberate, and that no simple identification was ever intended. Others have propounded composite interpretations so complex that they attribute to the prophet either a profound subtlety of mind or an inability to express his meaning clearly. There is, however, a further possibility: it may be that of the various features of the Servant portrayed here only one set is directly descriptive, while the others are allusive and intended to present him as embodying in his person all that was positive in Israel's earlier traditions. The problem remains: which of these features describes the real Servant?

The Servant is represented in the Songs as an individual person who acts, speaks and suffers and who is addressed by God and referred to by himself and others in individual terms, expressed as singular verbs and pronouns. But how much of this language is to be understood in a literal sense? Poetical language is very frequently figurative; and in the poems of the Old Testament nations and smaller human groups are commonly spoken of in terms of personification: that is, they are spoken of as if they were one single individual. This device is not confined to the use of the names of eponymous ancestors like Israel, Judah and Jacob to designate the nation. Ezekiel, for example, personified Samaria and Jerusalem as two women, Oholah and Oholibah (Ezek. 23). Outside the Servant Songs Deutero-Isaiah himself frequently used this device. He not only addressed the Babylonian exiles as 'Zion,' portrayed as a wife and mother, but he also, as has been seen, applied to them the term 'Yahweh's Servant.' One of the fundamental questions, therefore, with regard to the Servant in the Songs, is whether these four passages are an exception in this respect: whether here and only here the Servant is to be understood literally as an individual man, or whether here also the figure is a personification of the nation Israel or at least of some part of Israel.

Collective interpretations

The view that the Servant is *a personification of the people of Israel* is a very ancient one which continues to find support among contemporary scholars (e.g. de Boer, Snaith). Apart from the explicit identification in 49:3 (see below), its main strength lies in the resemblance between the events of the Servant's career—call, special status before Yahweh, suffering, imminent restoration and (according to one interpretation) mission to the world—and the history of Israel pictured by Deutero-Isaiah elsewhere in his oracles. Its adherents also claim for it the advantage of simplicity: the Servant's identity remains the same throughout the oracles. Deutero-Isaiah, however, did not, it seems, elsewhere regard such simplicity as a virtue, but rather delighted in applying the same epithets to quite different persons in different oracles, e.g. to Israel (43:1) and Cyrus (45:3, 4).

A number of objections can be raised against the identification of the Servant with Israel.

1. In 49:5-6 the Servant refers to a divine commission which he has received to restore Israel's fortunes. This is a difficult concept if the Servant and Israel are identical. Again in 53:1-6 the speakers ('we') refer to the things which the Servant ('he') has done for them. Who are the 'we'? The view that they are the foreign nations and kings mentioned in 52:15 is difficult to reconcile with their confession in 53:4-6, which appears to imply that they are representatives, or at least members, of the people of Israel. But if this is so, the Servant cannot himself be the embodiment of the nation.

2. In the Songs the Servant is represented as completely devoted to the service of Yahweh and as a wholly innocent sufferer. This is in marked contrast with what Deutero-Isaiah (not to speak of earlier prophets) says elsewhere about Israel, which according to him has thoroughly deserved its punishment. If the Servant of the Songs were a personification of the nation, Deutero-Isaiah's whole message would appear inconsistent.

3. Apart from the word 'Israel' in 49:3, to be discussed below, the Servant is never named in the Songs. It appears to be taken for granted that his identity is known to those addressed. Such an absence of identification by name is extremely rare in Old Testament passages in which a corporate entity is personified. But particularly significant is the absence of such identification in the two Songs (49:1-6 and 50:4-9) in which the Servant himself is the speaker. In the prophetical

books it may be assumed that speech in the first person singular other than that of Yahweh is that of the prophet himself, unless the contrary is specifically indicated by the naming of another speaker in an introductory phrase (e.g., 'But Zion said,' 49:14) or in the body of the speech, or by the context. That a personified Israel should be the speaker in these two Songs without any such specific indication is therefore improbable.

Against these objections must be weighed the occurrence of the word 'Israel' in 49:3. This text reads: 'And he said to me, "You are my servant, Israel, in whom I shall be glorified".' If the word 'Israel' here belongs to the original text, the identity of the Servant is clear. But there is some reason to suspect that it may be a gloss, that is, a comment by an early reader of the Book of Isaiah which later became incorporated into the text. If this were the case it would constitute an early, and not necessarily correct, *interpretation* of the identity of the Servant. It is curious that it occurs precisely in a passage (49:1-6) which otherwise provides some of the clearest evidence against his identification with Israel. There are several criteria which may be employed in determining whether the word is a gloss.

a. *The context*. Both in this and in the final Song the Servant is represented as standing apart from the corporate entity of Israel, having a task to perform on its behalf. This contextual argument does not, however, by itself constitute an adequate basis for textual emendation.

b. *Grammar and metrics*. Here the evidence is ambiguous. Neither the syntax nor the metre would be either seriously impaired or improved by the omission of the word 'Israel.'

c. *Textual variation*. All the ancient Versions agree with the standard Hebrew text in containing the word 'Israel.' One late Hebrew manuscript, however (Kenn 96), lacks it. Much discussion has taken place about the possibility that this may be not simply a careless omission by the scribe who made this copy of the Book of Isaiah, but an original reading which had come down to him and which he preserved.

d. *The existence of other similar interpretative glosses*. If 'Israel' is a gloss expressing a particular interpretation and not part of the original text, it does not stand alone, for two other glosses of precisely the same type occur in some manuscripts of the Greek (Septuagint) text of 42:1, which is part of the first Servant Song: there, whereas the

Hebrew text has simply 'my servant' and 'my chosen one,' the Greek text has '*Jacob* my servant' and 'my chosen one, *Israel*.' Here the words 'Jacob' and 'Israel,' which if original would seriously have overloaded the metre in the version of the Hebrew text which lies behind the Greek translation, are universally regarded as glosses. Although these examples are extant only in the Greek text, they witness to the existence of early glosses offering interpretations of the identity of the Servant in precisely this group of passages, and thus greatly strengthen the theory that 'Israel' in the Hebrew text of 49:3 is a gloss of the same type.

The difficulties attending the simple identification of the Servant in the Songs with Israel led some scholars (e.g. S.R. Driver, Skinner, Blank) to suggest that he stands for *a section of the nation*: a righteous remnant, 'ideal Israel,' or something similar. Such a righteous group would have been specially chosen by Yahweh as his agent in the redemption of the great mass of sinful Israel. Although this type of theory may at first seem plausible and would resolve some of the difficulties set out above, it is difficult to point to a single text in Deutero-Isaiah which clearly speaks of such a distinction within the nation.

An attempt was made by H.W. Robinson and O. Eissfeldt (1932-3), working separately, to reconcile the portrayal of the Servant as an individual with the corporate features observable both in the Songs and outside, by means of the concept which Robinson called *corporate personality*. According to this theory, which Robinson applied also to other aspects of Hebrew thought, the prophet's 'primitive psychology' enabled him to speak now of himself and now of Israel as the Servant of Yahweh: 'The Servant can be both the prophet himself as representative of the nation, and the nation whose proper mission is actually being fulfilled only by the prophet and that group of followers who may share his views' (Robinson). Whatever truth there may be in this hypothesis—and the validity of the concept of corporate personality as a way of describing the mentality of ancient Israel has been seriously questioned—it ought probably not to be classified, as is frequently done, as a corporate theory but rather as a variation of that in which the Servant is interpreted in the Songs as being the prophet himself.

The most recent of the corporate theories is that of Eaton, who, while pointing to certain supposed *royal* characteristics of the Servant in the Songs, believes that he stands, not for any individual king, but for the *Davidic dynasty*. His theory depends on the view that the pre-exilic autumnal festival as celebrated in Judah had included a rite in which the Davidic king was ritually humiliated and then restored to his throne. This theme, together with others drawn from the festival, was used in Deutero-Isaiah's oracles as a symbol of the fate of the whole Davidic dynasty: after a period of divine favour it had been humiliated by the Exile, but was about to be restored by Yahweh. The main message of the book is the coming restoration of the nation, after humiliation, by a divine act of salvation; and the restoration of the Davidic monarchy is an integral part and symbol of this restoration. Apart from its dependence on a particular and disputed interpretation of the autumn festival, this theory makes two assumptions which need further substantiation: that the Servant of the Songs is in fact primarily described in royal terms; and that the fate of the Davidic dynasty (explicitly referred to only in 55:3-4) played a significant role in the thought of Deutero-Isaiah as a whole.

Individual interpretations

The wealth and variety of the imagery employed in the Songs to describe the Servant's character and role have provided the basis for a wide range of interpretations of the figure as an individual. Different scholars have seen him as a new Moses, as a prophet, as a teacher of the law and as much else besides. Moreover the temporal imprecision of the modes of the Hebrew verb especially in poetical language has also made it uncertain whether the Servant, if he is an individual, was a contemporary of Deutero-Isaiah or a figure yet to come. Some phrases in the Songs have even suggested to some interpreters that he is a figure from the *earlier* history of Israel such as Moses or Jeremiah. However, such figures from the past could clearly not have occupied a central place in Deutero-Isaiah's message to his contemporaries. The phrases in question can only have been intended to contribute to the picture of the Servant by seeing him as a '*new* Moses,' a '*new* Jeremiah' or the like. Thus von Rad, for example, believed that the prophet looked forward to a future Servant who would be a prophet 'like Moses' but greater than he.

The view that the Songs are predictions of a figure who has not yet appeared has very ancient roots in the history of both Jewish and Christian interpretation. During the present century it has been given new life (especially by Gressmann, Engnell and Nyberg) as a consequence of the study of ancient Near Eastern myths, especially the myth of the dying and rising god and its supposed re-enactment in fertility cults. It is supposed—to take one version of this type of theory—that the description in chapter 53 of the humiliation and subsequent restoration of the Servant is a prediction of a Messianic figure, whose career and functions are expressed in terms derived from the sequence of events in the cultic myth of Tammuz. This myth could have been familiar to Deutero-Isaiah either directly through Babylonian sources or through Canaanizing elements in the pre-exilic cult of Jerusalem. (It should be noted that this type of theory can equally be used in conjunction with the view that the Servant is the nation Israel.) Theories of this kind have however lost support in recent years because the evidence both for the existence of a cult of a dying and rising god and for influence of this kind on the Israelite cult of Yahweh now appears very fragile (though Eaton's recent defence of it should be noted).

The projection of the Servant entirely into the future involves other difficulties. It might be possible to interpret 42:1-4 as a prophetic anticipation of the commissioning by Yahweh of a Servant who has yet to appear; but it is difficult to interpret 49:1-6 and 50:4-9, in which the Servant himself speaks of his past tribulations, in this way. Even less does chapter 53 make sense as a prophetic prediction of a wholly future series of events. Unless *some* of the events described here are events which had already taken place and were known to Deutero-Isaiah's audience, such detailed prediction could hardly have had any relevance to their own situation.

Deutero-Isaiah as the Servant

There remains the possibility that the Servant was a contemporary of Deutero-Isaiah, well known to him and to his audience. Duhm, Mowinckel (at one time) and more recently G.R. Driver believed that he was an *anonymous contemporary of the author of the Songs* of whom no mention is made elsewhere in the Old Testament. It would, however, be strange if a person so remarkable and so important to the author of the Songs had remained anonymous and had left no other memorial. However, if the Servant was a member of Deutero-Isaiah's own generation, there is an alternative possibility: that he was none other than *the prophet himself*. If this were so, the Songs would occupy a similar place in the body of the prophecies to that occupied in other prophetical books—notably the Book of Jeremiah—by reports of personal messages from Yahweh to the prophet, dialogues between Yahweh and the prophet, and narratives about the prophet. This view, which is a very ancient one, is that of a number of scholars today including von Waldow, Fohrer, Kutsch, Orlinsky, Schoors and Whybray.

What evidence do the Songs offer in support of this theory? The evidence that the Servant was a prophet is strong. In 42:1-4 the terms in which Yahweh affirms his choice of the Servant, promises to support him in his assigned task, and assures him of success despite opposition suggest the commissioning of a prophet and are strongly reminiscent of the calls of Jeremiah (1:8, 17-19) and of Ezekiel (2:3-7; 3:4-11). Again, like Jeremiah (1:5, 10) the Servant is to be Yahweh's instrument in the establishment of his sovereignty over the nations. This Song, however is not the call-narrative (which is found in 40:1-8) but a subsequent oracle confirming the prophet's claim to speak with Yahweh's authority.

In 49:1-6 the Servant's claim to have been called and chosen before his birth again echoes that of Jeremiah (1:5). A further prophetic feature is that Yahweh has made the Servant's mouth like a sharp sword (compare Jer. 1:9; Ezek. 3:2-3, 27), since it is the prophet's speech which is his most characteristic function. Finally the Servant's subsequent sense of failure, followed by a renewal of confidence in Yahweh's support, closely parallels the experiences of Jeremiah (e.g. 20:7-12).

In 50:4-9, where the opposition to the Servant has turned to active hostility and persecution, the resemblance to the experiences of Jeremiah (e.g. 11:18-23; 15:15-18; 18:18-23; 20:7-12) is even closer. Further, the opening words of this Song, in which the Servant describes himself as a pupil of Yahweh who learns from him how to speak words of comfort to the weary, strongly suggest the role of a prophet.

In 52:13-53:12 it may be inferred from the astonishment of the speakers (53:1) that an even later stage in the career of the Servant has been reached. After passing through such intense suffering and humiliation that he was regarded by others as singled out by Yahweh for especial punishment (verses 2-4), he has now in some unexpected way been rescued by the intervention of the 'arm of Yahweh.' The allusive language of the Song makes it impossible to be sure what was the nature of this rescue; but if, as may now be reasonably supposed, the prophetic figure of the Songs is Deutero-Isaiah himself, it may be conjectured that it was release from a Babylonian prison consequent on the fall of Babylon to Cyrus, which he had predicted. Even here there is a parallel with the career of Jeremiah, who (Jer. 40:1-6) had similarly predicted the fall of Jerusalem and was released by the Babylonians when they captured the city. If this interpretation is correct, this last Song is not the word of the prophet himself but was composed by his friends or disciples to express their thanks for his miraculous deliverance and at the prospect of his future prosperity and happiness.

Not all the scholars who identify the Servant with Deutero-Isaiah himself accept the above interpretation of the final Song. The traditional view that the Song was composed after his death by his followers still commands support. 53:7-9 are held to refer to his death, while 53:10b-12 promise his future resurrection.

It is undoubtedly possible to interpret verses 7-9 as a literal description of the prophet's death. Such an interpretation, however, does not take account of the way in which the language of death is used in Israelite psalms of lamentation and thanksgiving, a category to which this Song belongs. In some of these psalms (e.g. Ps. 22:15; 88:4-6) the psalmist, in describing the severe sickness or other calamitous state into which he had fallen, used language which if interpreted literally would mean that he was actually dead. It is therefore possible that the speakers in 53:7-9, referring to the prophet's previous extreme danger, used the same kind of language.

But even if these verses are interpreted literally the references to death are not as clear as they might at first seem to be. We may discount the reference to the 'lamb to the slaughter' in verse 7, since this is manifestly no more than a simile and is in fact used also by Jeremiah (11:19) with reference to his own, non-fatal, sufferings. But even the expressions 'taken away' and 'cut off from the land of the living' (verse 8) may refer simply to confinement in prison; the preparation of the grave in verse 9 probably refers not to actual burial but to the gleeful anticipation of the prophet's death by his enemies (compare Ps. 35:25; 41:5, 8; 88:4-5); the phrase 'in his death' in the same verse is now universally regarded (see the Jerusalem Bible and the NEB) as a corrupt reading; and 'poured out his life to death' in verse 12 probably means 'risked his life' rather than 'died.' This interpretation of these verses, which is supported by Orlinsky,

G.R. Driver, Soggin and Whybray (1978), is strengthened by the fact that verses 10b-12, which speak of the prophet's happy future, nowhere hint at a restoration to life after death, which would be a most unlikely belief in the sixth century B.C., but are most naturally interpreted as speaking of a dramatic change for the better in the prophet's fortunes after his terrible experiences.

Against the identification of the Servant with Deutero-Isaiah—or indeed with any merely human figure—it has been argued that the Servant's character and role, especially as described in chapter 53, far transcend those conceivable of ordinary humanity. To this it may be replied that the concept of prophecy in the Old Testament—for example, in the Book of Jeremiah—is an exceptionally exalted one. Only in one respect could it be plausibly maintained that the Servant transcends this: in his supposed role of 'vicarious sufferer.' Certain phrases in the final Song (in 53:4-6, the final line of 8b, and 10-12) have been interpreted in traditional Christian exegesis as stating that the Servant suffered vicariously for others: that is, that through his own unmerited suffering he enabled others to escape the divine punishment which they had deserved. This is still the view of many scholars; but it has recently been questioned (Orlinsky, Whybray).

It would indeed be astonishing if these verses stated that the prophet had suffered so that his fellow-exiles might go scot-free. For in fact they had not gone scot-free, and, as has already been noted, Deutero-Isaiah's message depended to a large extent on this fact: the people had already suffered, and suffered in full, for their sins. Moreover, Yahweh had now pronounced their forgiveness. No vicarious suffering, therefore, was required. Apart from this, the idea of vicarious suffering, as Orlinsky has shown, is totally alien to Old Testament belief. For Yahweh to accept the punishment of the innocent and to acquit the guilty would be an unthinkable infringement of the principle, maintained consistently throughout the Old Testament, that 'He who justifies the wicked and he who condemns the righteous are both alike an abomination to Yahweh' (Prov. 17:15).

What, then, is the meaning of such phrases as 'he makes himself a sin-offering' (53:10), 'upon him was the chastisement that makes us whole' (53:5) and 'he bore the sin of many' (53:12)? The statement that the Servant became a sacrificial victim ('āšām, 'sin-offering') has greatly influenced the christological interpretation of the Servant; but the whole of the first part of this verse is extremely corrupt in the Hebrew and virtually unintelligible. It would be wrong to base any serious conclusions about the role of the Servant on it. If in fact it did make the Servant into a human sacrifice acceptable to Yahweh by equating him with an animal sacrifice, this would be totally contrary to the principles of the religion of Yahweh as understood in the Old Testament.

The other statements referred to above must be understood in the context of the life and times of Deutero-Isaiah. It is clear (e.g. from 53:9b) that he was an exceptionally righteous man and that his exceptional sufferings were undeserved. They were caused solely by the fact that he had accepted the prophetic office and so undertaken the proclamation of a politically dangerous message: the prophecy of the fall of Babylon. He thus 'bore the sins of many' not in the sense of suffering instead of the many—which, as we have noted, was not the case—but of enduring additional and exceptional suffering. This suffering, as in the case of other prophets, was the consequence of the nation's sin, for it was the nation's plight which had made his prophetic activity necessary. At the same time it could be said that his sufferings led to their restoration to 'wholeness' or their 'healing'—that is, to their release from exile: for had he not persevered in his dangerous work at the risk of suffering and death, the divine word which, like a sharp sword in Yahweh's hand, brought about the fall of Babylon would not have been pronounced.

The portrait of the Servant of Yahweh which emerges from the Songs on the basis of the above interpretation is not one of a person who transcends ordinary humanity, but of an exceptionally faithful prophet of Yahweh who, like his predecessor Jeremiah, endured great suffering in the course of his ministry but also experienced the intervention of Yahweh on his behalf to deliver him from danger. His ministry was entirely bound up with the life of his people, and it may well be that his rescue from death was regarded by those who composed chapter 53 as the turning-point in the fortunes of their community.

Evaluation of Deutero-Isaiah's Message

The bright future which Deutero-Isaiah held out to his fellow-exiles was conceived and expressed in concrete terms, not as a distant hope but as an imminent reality. His picture of the future life of the nation after its restoration to its homeland was indeed of a life lived under ideal conditions; but there is no apocalyptic cataclysm here, no new heaven and earth. The fantastic speculations of some of the later prophets (not to speak of the apocalyptists) are wholly absent: there is, for example, no unnatural fertility such as is predicted in Amos 9:13, no abrogation of the functions of sun and moon as in Isa. 60:19-20, and no miraculous river flowing from the restored Jerusalem as in Ezek. 47. The picture is essentially a sober one involving no essential change in the conditions of life.

In order to establish this new state of affairs there will indeed be a miraculous intervention; but this will not differ in principle from the marvellous deeds already performed by Yahweh in the past. Indeed, the sequence of events anticipated—overthrow of the tyrant, release of the captives, march through the desert, miraculous provision of food and drink, settlement and reconstruction, dominance over the nations—is clearly modelled on the historical traditions of Israel's earlier progress from exodus to empire. The 'new things' will certainly be even more glorious than the 'former things'; but they will not be different in kind.

When Israel is restored to its land its enemies will be eliminated (41:11-12; 54:15-17) and the nations will come to do homage (45:14; 49:7, 22-23); Jerusalem and its temple will be restored to a state more glorious than before (44:28; 49:16-17; 54:11-12), and Israel will be the envy of the world (44:5). Both city and land will enjoy a wonderful prosperity, with a large and thriving population (49:17-21; 51:3). Much of this picture is derived from a combination of the themes of the fulfilment of the promises to Abraham and of the restoration of the glories of the reign of David. There will, however, be one new feature: Yahweh's favour and blessing, once restored, will never again be taken away from his chosen people. The life of blessedness will be eternal (45:17; 54:10, 15-17).

This is a remarkable expectation; but it is not an apocalyptic one. Deutero-Isaiah believed that Yahweh intended shortly to bring about a fundamental change in the political scene which would somehow bring Israel to dominance. How this would be done is not clear: no connection is made in the oracles between these predictions and the role of Cyrus. But this is clearly what he expected to happen. The fact that it did not happen constitutes a major problem in the evaluation of Deutero-Isaiah as a prophet.

Some of Deutero-Isaiah's expectations were admittedly fulfilled. Cyrus did conquer Babylon and permit the exiled peoples to return to their homes. The temple at Jerusalem was rebuilt, though only on a modest scale and after an interval of some twenty years. (The restoration of the city itself was delayed for more than a hundred years.) But there was no massive, triumphant return of the exiles, no new and more glorious Exodus, no miraculous journey across the desert. Few, it seems, took immediate advantage of the permission to return home: many preferred to remain. Life for those who did return was hard; and prosperity did not return until several generations had passed. Above all, there was no return to the glories of David's reign, or even to political independence. Never again until modern times was there to be an independent Jewish state, except for a brief period four centuries after the time of Deutero-Isaiah. We learn, indeed, from the literature of the early post-exilic period—Trito-Isaiah, Malachi, Zechariah, Haggai—that the failure of expectations such as those which Deutero-Isaiah had promoted constituted one of the greatest problems of that time.

Was Deutero-Isaiah, then, a false prophet? Some modern scholars, notably Torrey, rejected the entire hypothesis of an exilic 'Deutero-Isaiah' because they believed that it entails such a conclusion. It would be absurd, they argued, to suppose that the oracles of a 'prophet' so utterly discredited by the failure of his prophecies would have been preserved by succeeding generations and enshrined in the canon. Isa. 40-55 must be accounted for in some other way.

None of the alternatives proposed by Torrey or by others has, however, been able to shake the consensus of modern scholarship that the oracles contained in these chapters are the words of an exilic prophet. The arguments supporting this consensus, which have been briefly set out in this book, remain valid. The solution to the problem is to be found rather in the nature of Hebrew prophecy itself. If Hebrew prophecy were the art of accurate and detailed prediction of the future there would be little true prophecy in the Old Testament. But this is not the case. Prediction of the future was only a small part of the prophetic task, as the prophetic call-narratives, including that of Deutero-Isaiah, testify. Deutero-Isaiah did not fail to comfort his people by proclaiming the message which he had heard in the heavenly council that Yahweh had pardoned his people and that their time of punishment was ended (40:1-2); and this was a true message. It was the word which the nation needed to hear at one of the greatest crises in its history, when its very existence as a people was in the balance. The fact that the Jewish people and their faith survived, and survived alone among the peoples and religions of the ancient Near East is due to the tenacity of their sense of being Yahweh's chosen people and to the firmness and maturity of their faith. By stimulating that sense of being the people of God, and by deepening that faith through his teaching and his personal example, Deutero-Isaiah played a crucial role in ensuring that survival, and so fully deserves recognition as a true prophet who faithfully proclaimed the word of God.

Further Reading

On Deutero-Isaiah's teaching in general see:

*S.H. Blank, *Prophetic Faith in Isaiah*, London: A. & C. Black, 1958 / Wayne State University Press, 1967, chapters 4-9

*P.A.H. de Boer, *Second Isaiah's Message* (Oudtestamentische Studiën, 11), Leiden: Brill, 1956

*J.H. Eaton, *Festal Drama in Deutero-Isaiah*, London: SPCK, 1979

*Muilenburg, 398-406

*Von Rad (1968), chapter 17 (or *Theology* II, 238-62)

*N.H. Snaith, 'Isaiah 40-66. A Study of the Teaching of the Second Isaiah and its Consequences,' in H.M. Orlinsky and N.H. Snaith, *Studies in the Second Part of the Book of Isaiah* (VT Suppl. 14), Leiden: Brill, 1967 (reprinted 1977), 135-264

*Von Waldow (1968)

For a full account of the various interpretations of the Servant of Yahweh see especially:

*C.R. North, *The Suffering Servant in Deutero-Isaiah. An Historical and Critical Study*, Oxford: Oxford University Press, 1948

As examples of some different interpretations of the Servant Songs, see:

D.J.A. Clines, *I, He, We and They: A Literary Approach to Isaiah 53* (JSOT Supplement Series, 1), Sheffield: JSOT Press, 1976

G.R. Driver, 'Isaiah 52,13 – 53,12: the Servant of the Lord,' in *In Memoriam Paul Kahle*, BZAW 103 (1968), 90-105

*O. Eissfeldt, 'The Ebed-Yahwe in Isaiah xl-lv in the Light of the Israelite Conceptions of the Community and the Individual, the Ideal and the Real,' *Expository Times* 44 (1932-3), 261-8

I. Engnell, 'The Ebed Yahweh Songs and the Suffering Messiah in

"Deutero-Isaiah",' *Bulletin of the John Rylands Library* 31 (1948), 54-93

J. Lindblom, *The Servant Songs in Deutero-Isaiah. A New Attempt to Solve an Old Problem*, Lund: Gleerup, 1951

*S. Mowinckel, *He That Cometh*, Oxford: Basil Blackwell, 1956, chapter 7

*Muilenburg, 406-14

*H.M. Orlinsky, 'The So-Called "Servant of the Lord" and "Suffering Servant" in Second Isaiah,' in Orlinsky and Snaith, 1-133 (see under N.H. Snaith above)

*H.W. Robinson, *The Cross of the Servant*, London: SCM Press, 1925, reprinted in H.W. Robinson, *The Cross in the Old Testament*, London: SCM Press, 1955, 55-114

H.H. Rowley, 'The Servant of the Lord in the Light of Three Decades of Criticism,' in H.H. Rowley, *The Servant of the Lord and Other Essays on the Old Testament*, London: Lutterworth Press, 1952, 1-57

R.N. Whybray, *Thanksgiving for a Liberated Prophet. An Interpretation of Isaiah Chapter 53* (JSOT Supplement Series, 4), Sheffield: JSOT Press, 1978

Other essays on various topics in Deutero-Isaiah include:

B.W. Anderson, 'Exodus Typology in Second Isaiah,' in B.W. Anderson and W. Harrelson (ed.), *Israel's Prophetic Heritage. Essays in Honor of James Muilenburg*, London: SCM Press / New York: Harper and Row, 1962, 177-95

F.M. Cross, 'The Council of Yahweh in Second Isaiah,' *Journal of Near Eastern Studies* 12 (1953), 274-7

C.R. North, 'The "Former Things" and the "New Things" in Deutero-Isaiah,' in H.H. Rowley (ed.), *Studies in Old Testament Prophecy Presented to T.H. Robinson*, Edinburgh: T. & T. Clark, 1950, 111-26

*G. von Rad, 'The Theological Problem of the Old Testament Doctrine of Creation,' in G. von Rad, *The Problem of the Hexateuch and Other Essays*, Edinburgh and London: Oliver and Boyd, 1966, 131-43

INDEX OF SUBJECTS

INDEX OF AUTHORS